"*Sunday School That Really Responds* is your 911 call for help. Sooner or later every Sunday school will have these issues, and when yours does, you will be glad you bought this book. This book is organized so you can go right to the section you need for immediate help and practical ideas. Steve Parr has shown hundreds of Sunday schools how to diagnose problems and implement solutions. With this book, he can help yours as well."

—*Josh Hunt*
Author of *You Can Double Your Sunday School in Two Years or Less*

"Sunday school plays a vital role in churches across America. While curricula abounds, practical helps for the everyday questions of Sunday school workers are much rarer. Steve Parr has provided an outstanding tool to answer the questions every Sunday school teacher or leader asks at one point or another. I commend it to you."

—*Alvin L. Reid*
Professor of Evangelism and Student Ministry,
Bailey Smith Chair of Evangelism,
Southeastern Baptist Theological Seminary

"There are two features that make *Sunday School That Really Responds* a valuable resource. Parr's work is both functional and faithful. The content and the structure of each chapter make it an ideal reference tool that addresses specific issues faced in local congregations. Throughout Parr is faithful to Scripture, acknowledging from the outset that nothing of significance happens in our churches apart from the presence of the power of the Holy Spirit."

—*Mark H. Crumpler*
Pastor for Teaching and Spiritual Formation,
Peachtree Presbyterian Church, Atlanta, GA

"Steve Parr has provided a comprehensive 411 on the most common 911s encountered by Sunday school leaders and teachers. The book has a creative format that makes it the perfect addition to any Sunday school leader's bookshelf. You may not need to know right now about all 24 of the challenges he identifies, but you probably will eventually! So buy it. Read it. Or just focus on the parts that pertain to the emergency you're facing right now. Then put it somewhere that's easy to find. You'll need it again!"

—*David Francis*
Director of Sunday School and Discipleship, Lifeway Church Resources

"Oftentimes an author dwells on the theoretical aspect of his topic but gives very little help in meeting needs. Not so with Steve Parr! This book is crammed full of practical wisdom that will actually help your Sunday school become what you envision. As a Sunday school leader, you now have a tool that will equip you to respond to your needs in a most competent way. You will refer often to this book."

—*Allan Taylor*
Minister of Education, First Baptist Church of Woodstock, GA

"A quick scan of the table of contents reveals perhaps the most relevant list of Sunday school challenges you have ever seen. As you venture into the book, you will be delighted with the way Steve Parr addresses these issues. This book is a practical and helpful manual you will consult from time to time as a Sunday school or church staff leader."

—*J. Robert White*
Executive Director, Georgia Baptist Convention

"Pastor: you, your staff, and lay leaders will greatly appreciate Steve Parr's insight and information on Sunday school and evangelism. Sunday school is the heartbeat of the church for the caring and keeping of all its members as well as a vital tool for reaching out to the unchurched. This book will motivate and encourage you while pointing you in the right direction."

—*Bobby Welch*
Retired Pastor of First Baptist Church of Daytona Beach, FL,
Strategist for Global Evangelical Relations of SBC

Sunday School
That Really
Responds

Wisdom for
Confronting 24
Common Sunday
School Emergencies

Steve R. Parr

Kregel
Academic & Professional

Sunday School That Really Responds: Wisdom for Confronting 24 Common Sunday School Emergencies

© 2011 Steve R. Parr

Published by Kregel Publications, a division of Kregel, Inc., P.O. Box 2607, Grand Rapids, MI 49501.

Library of Congress Cataloging-in-Publication Data
Parr, Steve R., 1958-
  Sunday school that really responds : wisdom for confronting 24 common Sunday school emergencies / Steve R. Parr.
    p. cm.
  1. Sunday schools. I. Title.
  BV1521.3.P37 2011
  268'.1—dc23

                                                          2011024222

ISBN 978-0-8254-4064-9

Printed in the United States of America
11 12 13 14 15 / 5 4 3 2 1

To Leah, Lauren, and Larissa,
my three awesome daughters,
who give me joy, support, and encouragement.
I thank the Lord for your lives and your love.

To Leah, Lauren, and Larissa,
my three awesome daughters,
who give me joy, support, and encouragement.
I thank the Lord for your lives and your love.

CONTENTS

FOREWORD

I DO SUNDAY SCHOOL TRAINING for a living. After I present a talk on *You Can Double Your Class in Two Years or Less*, someone invariably will come up to me with a question. They might ask one of the following:

- How can we get people to step up and serve?

- How can we get teachers to participate in training?

- Our teaching is boring; what can we do?

- We don't have space to double. What advice do you have for us?

As we are talking, I realize a couple things:

- I didn't address this particular issue.

- If this issue is not addressed, it can single-handedly kill the potential growth of the Sunday school.

I sometimes wish I had ten hours to address all the things that can keep a Sunday school from growing. But would that amount of time be enough? And, even if I had that amount of time, I would have to deal with a lot of individualized problems. Some churches might love to hear about creative ways to provide more space. For others, this is the least of their worries. A lot of churches could triple in size with the existing room that they have.

It would be great if there was a resource that would address all the potential problems that churches have with their Sunday schools in one concise volume. Then, when you had an issue with space or leadership or training or whatever, you could quickly and easily find the answer. That volume is now before you.

Steve Parr knows Sunday school. He has helped hundreds of Sunday schools through the process of diagnosing problems and implementing solutions. He has helped hundreds of dying Sunday schools back to health, and with this volume he can help yours as well.

I have heard voiced every one of the problems that Steve addresses here. These are not theoretical; if you are not facing one of these situations now, you probably soon will be. Steve provides practical solutions to common dilemmas and addresses them in a practical, creative, and interesting way.

This volume is a great contribution to the literature on Sunday school and should be on the shelf of every pastor, Minister of Education, Sunday school director, and Sunday school teacher. My advice is to read it through in its entirety, then keep it handy—you will need it.

—Josh Hunt, author of
*You Can Double Your Class
in Two Years or Less* and
Make Your Group Grow

ACKNOWLEDGMENTS

THE RESPONSE TO MY FIRST book with Kregel Publications, *Sunday School That Really Works*, has been fantastic! Thanks to so many of you who have utilized the book both for equipping leaders and for developing your personal leadership.

My life and ministry are the result of many influences. Once again, I am grateful for the support of Dr. J. Robert White and the staff of the Georgia Baptist Convention. Dr. White encourages staff members to write and to grow to their fullest potential. I am a beneficiary of that philosophy, and I am indebted to the Georgia Baptist Convention for the role that the leadership and the staff have played in giving me the freedom and resources to pursue this project in addition to my ministry responsibilities.

I am grateful for many encouragers who shaped and influenced my leadership in the earliest stages of my spiritual journey. I want to express thanks to Lamoyne Sharpe and the congregation of First Baptist Church in Dacula, Georgia, for their investment in my childhood years. Pastor Mike Soop and the members of New Canaan Baptist Church in Lawrenceville, Georgia, have always been dear to my heart, because their affirmation of my mission and ministry influenced my leadership perhaps more than any other factor. I cannot say enough for the Hebron Baptist Church in Dacula, Georgia, and the former pastor of that congregation, the Reverend Larry Wynn, for his investment in my leadership and for the skills that I learned from him in over fourteen years of partnership and more than two decades of friendship. All of my current and former staff members have helped in my growth, but none more than

Dr. Tim Smith and Dr. Alan Folsom. I also want to pay tribute to Lucy Henry, who is retiring after thirteen years of service as my administrative assistant.

I am blessed with a godly heritage of grandparents, twelve sets of aunts and uncles, and dozens of cousins—some living and some who are with the Lord—who have encouraged, invested their lives, and loved me. Thanks to each and every one of you for your role in and influence on my life. My parents, Ben and Betty Parr; my sister, Michelle Watson; my wife, Carolyn; and my daughters, to whom this book is dedicated, touch my life each and every day. I am indeed a blessed man.

I am thankful for the excellent staff at Kregel Publications. They have been a blessing to me, and God is using the staff to touch many lives through the publication of excellent Christian books and resources. You are a blessing to leaders like me who desire to maximize their influence for the cause of Christ. I also want to say a special thanks to my daughter, Lauren, for assisting with the editing and formatting of this project in preparation for the publisher.

Most of all, I am thankful to God for His blessings and provision. It is only by His grace and power that I can accomplish anything at all. It is ultimately to His glory that I present this book and myself.

Get Ready to Respond

NINE-ONE-ONE

You never want to have to dial 911, but are grateful that it is available when needed. You can dial the number from 98 percent of the phones in North America and receive an immediate response from an operator who will diagnose the nature of your situation and accordingly dispatch a first responder to provide aid in your crisis. Police officers, fire fighters, or emergency medical personnel respond with urgency to provide you with much needed assistance. Sometimes their actions mean the difference between life and death. Men and women who serve in these first responder roles are well-trained, skilled, passionate about their work, and cool under pressure—exactly what is needed when a crisis strikes. I am sure you share my gratitude for these devoted public servants.

Have you ever had a crisis in your Sunday school ministry or the small group that you lead? It sure would be great if there was a first-responder system in place where you could call and get immediate assistance from someone with training and experience in Sunday school ministry. While it may not be feasible to have a nationwide system with 24/7 access by phone, it is possible to have a resource at hand that addresses some of the most common emergencies that you will face. You have in your hands a resource that I have entitled *Sunday School That Really Responds*—a guide to assist with twelve of the most common Sunday school emergencies faced by church leaders and twelve of the most common emergencies encountered by Sunday school teachers and group leaders.

Following First Responder 101 basic training, you will find two sections, each containing twelve Sunday school emergencies. The first section addresses the larger organizational issues faced by pastors, Sunday school directors, education ministers, and church staff. The second section focuses on the specifics faced in the smaller setting of a Sunday school class or small group by Sunday school teachers and small group leaders. Each of the twenty-four chapters is organized in the following manner.

The Emergency. The introductory section contains a story, illustration, anecdote, or humorous perspective on the *issue* at hand. While reading "the emergency" section of each chapter, you will find plenty of newsletter, sermon, or teaching material, along with immediate stress relief.

Triage. The second section of each chapter will help you to quickly *diagnose* the severity of the situation at hand. Five questions are posed that will help you quantify the severity of the emergency. Ideally, the answer to all five of the questions presented is "yes." The more times that you answer "no" to the questions, the more severe the emergency. You can find a tool for analysis on page 17 that will give you the range of severity. Answering "no" to only one of the five questions indicates that you have a minor injury and should "pay attention lest an infection begins to develop." Answering "no" to all five questions indicates a need for resuscitation: "You are fortunate to still be alive (that is, your Sunday school or class). Take action and expect long-term rehab to be required."

Prescription. The third section will offer three to five Scripture passages that will lay the foundation for the *biblical response* to the situation. These will be helpful in prayer, sermon preparation, or presentations for equipping leaders; and, most importantly, in seeking God's wisdom and guidance for responding to the emergencies you face.

First Aid. The fourth section of each chapter suggests the *immediate actions* that need to take place. Emergency personnel do not simply load patients into the ambulance and take them to the emergency room. They take immediate action to stabilize the patient, to provide some immediate relief if possible, and to minimize negative consequences. The ideas provided can be implemented and applied quickly to provide some relief to the situation and to begin the healing process.

Rehab. The final section of each chapter addresses the *longterm actions* that need to be implemented to resolve the problem and to reduce the chances of it recurring. Emergency patients are often admitted to the hospital for intensive care. The final section will provide the strategies you need to strengthen and heal your Sunday school ministry or class.

Sunday School That Really Responds can be used in several ways. You may want to read it chronologically from start to finish in order to enhance your knowledge and leadership skills. A second approach is to use the book as a reference guide, and go immediately to the chapter that addresses the emergency you are facing. A third way to use the book is as an equipping guide. You can read through it with a team or take a section at a time and use the material in your equipping time with Sunday school leaders or staff. *Sunday School That Really Responds* paired with *Sunday School That Really Works* will provide a wealth of material to help keep your Sunday school ministry healthy and growing.

TRIAGE DIAGNOSIS

EACH ISSUE ADDRESSED IN THE following chapters includes a five-question "Triage" section to assist you in evaluating and diagnosing the severity of the problems encountered in your Sunday school. After answering the triage questions in each chapter, evaluate the results using this guide.

How many questions did you answer with "no"?

One. You have a minor injury. Pay attention lest an infection begins to develop.

Two. You have a wound. You need to take immediate action to prevent further damage.

Three. You have a significant injury. Take it seriously or you could suffer long-term consequences.

Four. You are seriously injured. Failure to respond will be costly to you and to others around you.

Five. Break out the defibrillator. You (that is, your Sunday school or class) are fortunate to still be alive. Take action and expect long-term rehab to be required.

Sunday School First Responder 101

FIRST RESPONDERS AND EMERGENCY MEDICAL technicians go through hours of classroom and experiential training prior to their assignment to react to emergencies. Every professional needs to know the basic principles and practices of his or her assignment. Before addressing specific problems encountered by Sunday school leaders, you will do well to take some time to understand some of the basic principles that apply to any situation that you might encounter when it comes to Sunday school emergencies. Please take note of the following ten principles and plan to refer to them often in order to sharpen your leadership skills for responding to Sunday school emergencies.

Principle of Spiritual Biology. *Concepts will not solve issues in the absence of the working of the Holy Spirit.* No concept, principle, opinion, or word of advice that you will find in the following chapters is intended to supersede the necessity of God interceding by the power of His Spirit. Every challenge encountered in the body of Christ should be bathed with prayer, approached with Christlike boldness and gentleness, remain true to the Word of God, and dependent on godly wisdom. Spiritual problems require spiritual solutions. I pray that God will work through the wisdom and experiences that I share to speak to your heart and prepare you to address whatever challenges you might encounter as a leader in your congregation.

First responders understand how critical those first sixty minutes are after a person suffers an injury from an accident. This principle urges them to respond without delay. The "Golden Hour" refers to "the time period of one hour in which the lives of a majority of critically injured trauma patients can be saved if definitive surgical intervention is provided."[1] Dr. R. Adams Cowley reports that the mortality rate among patients who are treated within one hour is 10 percent. The mortality rate increases dramatically following that first hour and reaches 75 percent when treatment is delayed for eight or more hours.[2]

How does this apply to your Sunday school ministry? *The longer a response is delayed, the more likely it is for greater damage or even death to occur.* It is very important that you take time to answer the "triage" questions if you are facing one of the emergencies described in this book. If you can answer "yes" to at least four of the questions, then you may be able to stand back and let the situation resolve itself. Otherwise, some action is needed, and the more severe the problem the more quickly you need to respond. A delay will cause the damage to increase

---

1. "The Golden Hour," The NJ Trauma Center, The University Hospital, http://www.theuniversityhospital.com/trauma/gold.htm (accessed April 14, 2011).,

2. R. Adams Cowley cited at "The 'Golden Hour' In Transit," http://medteam. wordpress.com/2008/01/07/the-golden-hour-in-transit-%E2%80%93-proposed-nhs-%E2%80%9Crestructuring%E2%80%9D-targets-ae-and-maternity-care-with-dangerous-cuts-that-will-cost-lives/ (accessed 1 January 2011).

dramatically, and you may experience the loss of members or leaders.

Principle of Triage. Triage is the process of sorting injured people into groups based on their need for or likely benefit from immediate medical attention. It is the first step of diagnosis to determine the severity of the injury and the urgency of the treatment needed. You will need to take time to diagnose the problem at hand in order to respond with the appropriate amount of urgency. *You cannot solve a problem that you do not know how to diagnose.* Take time to evaluate the issue you are facing by considering the questions in the triage section of each chapter before responding. You do not want to overreact to a small problem and cause offense to a volunteer leader, and you do not want to delay in addressing a problem that may cause great damage to the reputation of your church because of a failure to respond. Take time to evaluate before determining the course of action. All problems are not equal in regard to severity but few tend to resolve themselves. Pray for wisdom and seek additional counsel when needed.

Principle of the Emergency Room. *Though the wait is long and the bill is high, the trip usually beats the alternative.* The emergency room is one of the last places in the world that I want to visit. No one goes to the emergency room for good news, entertainment, or a few hours of relaxation. The experience is often unpleasant for the patient as well as for family members and friends. However, there is another way to look at the emergency room: It is a place where healing begins. Be cautious not to ignore problems simply because dealing with them will be unpleasant. Do not let a minor ailment become an infection and perhaps even a disease that over time can destroy relationships and ministry. The sting of alcohol on a cut is preferable to an amputation resulting from an infection that grew out of neglect. Though the emergency room experience is not something to which you aspire, do not let fear or neglect cause a problem to worsen.

Principle of Anecdotal Trends. *Sunday schools do not succeed or fail because of what happens in churches other than their own.* You will do well to study, observe, and learn from other churches. You can often learn what to do and what not to do from the experiences of others. However, just because something worked in another church does not mean it will work in yours, and just because it failed in another does not mean it will fail in yours. Beware of either adopting or dismissing an idea based on an anecdotal trend that is found only in an individual church or a small group of churches. These anecdotal trends may receive wide publicity but may not reflect what is happening in churches other than that select few. I love research and I believe that you can learn a great deal to help you be more effective in your leadership, but be discerning in your evaluation of it. I see too many churches dismissing Sunday school and making decisions based on anecdotal trends instead of actual percentages and research that can be quite instructive.

Principle of Investment. *Small investments rarely result in large returns.* Most of the problems that you encounter in Sunday school do not lend themselves to quick fixes. You must invest weeks and months to change the culture of the Sunday school to get it to be healthy and growing. Do not expect to read a chapter, make a couple of calls, and resolve the problem in the next few days. That may happen occasionally, and you can be thankful if it does, but that will be the exception and not the rule. Consider this principle in the context of the overall health of your Sunday school as well. Sunday school will not function effectively on autopilot. Leaders must invest and provide consistent attention and training for it to be healthy. You will still encounter emergencies even when a higher investment is made; however, the problems will be minimized compared with those of a church that neglects or makes only small investments into the health of the Sunday school ministry.

Principle of the Expert. *Knowledge in a group will not rise above that of the key leader.* The greater your leadership role in your congregation, the more of this book you should take time to consume. The pastor is the expert among the congregation. The teacher is the expert in his or her class or group. You need to be as knowledgeable as possible to provide the leadership that God has called you to. Many if not most of the problems addressed in this book are the result of a lack of knowledge and training about the principles and tools of Sunday school health and growth. Your knowledge can help prevent future problems if you will share it with your volunteers through training opportunities. However, you cannot teach what you do not know.

Principle of Un-Omniscience. *No one can know everything, and sometimes assistance is needed from an experienced expert.* The book that you are reading is one step that you can take to get some objective guidance. However, do not be afraid to call a specialist. This often happens once a patient gets into the emergency room. A cardiologist, trauma specialist, neurologist, plastic surgeon, dentist, or some other specialist may be called upon because of the individual's special training and experience. You should learn and know as much as you can while understanding that every person has limitations. Do not hesitate to call in a specialist to assist you in evaluating and addressing the problems that you encounter.

Principle of Rehabilitation. *The length of the recovery is proportionate to the depth of the problem.* Please understand that you cannot resolve in a week what took a decade to develop.

Your congregation and your Sunday school ministry have developed a culture over the course of the past few years. Habits can be developed and entrenched which can be healthy or unhealthy. No problem is beyond resolution, but some take more time than others. The sections in each chapter on rehab are as important as the immediate responses. Failure to apply these principles will result in reoccurrence of the problem that has been encountered. The overall health of the Sunday school must be continually attended to, in addition to the isolated problem that you are addressing.

Principle of Gravitation. *Whatever the leader elevates is that to which the followers gravitate.* Is Sunday school a priority in your church? Is it viewed as important by your leaders and the congregation? If not, the problems that you have with Sunday school will only multiply. The pastor must elevate and support the Sunday school ministry verbally, passionately, and consistently. Failure to do so will only exacerbate the problems faced by the Sunday school leaders. Likewise, the Sunday school teachers and group leaders must believe in the priority of the Sunday school, not as a program but as a strategy to assist the church in faithful obedience to the Great Commission.

Now it is time to begin looking at specific problems encountered by Sunday school leaders and staff members. Please note that every paragraph could be a full chapter and every chapter could be a book. I can easily spend an hour providing instruction on any of the items mentioned. However, I must take advantage of time and space. Remember that the issues must always be addressed with prayer and godly wisdom. But, for now, this is *Sunday School That Really Responds*. What is the nature of your emergency?

PART 1

Common
Organizational
Emergencies

CHAPTER 1

Our Sunday School Is Dying

✚ THE EMERGENCY

Operator: You have reached the Sunday School First-Responder Hotline. This is officer Larissa speaking. What is the nature of your emergency, please?

Caller: Please! Somebody help us. It's our Sunday school.

Operator: What's wrong? Is everyone OK? Is someone injured?

Caller: No. It's our Sunday school. I think it's dying. Please, can someone help us?

Operator: Sir, remain calm. We're going to get you some help. Please stay on the line with me. Now, you said your Sunday school is dying. Perhaps there is still some life and some hope. Trust me. I've taken these calls before. Rest assured that others have been in this same predicament and we were able to help.

Caller: I think it's too late. Only a few people are attending and we have been in decline for months. I'm worried. People once came to our Sunday school to grow and to serve. We tried doubling the caffeine in the coffee and we even gave out high-energy drinks last month. It didn't work. Our Sunday school could be mistaken for a sleep lab if the proper equipment were in place. We used to have a lot of people attending and guests almost every Sunday. Now we are down to a faithful few and they are just barely hanging on.

Operator: Sir, it does sound severe. But, there *are* people remaining. More importantly, God is not done with you. You wouldn't have called if you didn't want help. It takes someone with concern to recognize what is going on and to be willing to take action.

Caller: Please help us. I don't want our Sunday school to die!

Operator: I hear you. And more importantly, God hears you. Does your Sunday school have a pulse?

Caller: Yes, but barely. Hold on. I think I hear the sirens.

Operator: Hold on tight, sir. First responders are on the way!

✚ TRIAGE

1. Is the average attendance at least slightly higher than it was at this same time last year?

2. Is the average attendance significantly higher than five years ago?

3. Is the enrollment significantly higher than it was three years ago?

4. Are a majority of your leaders enthusiastic about your Sunday school?

5. Are you regularly having guests visit in Sunday school?

Diagnosis: Refer to page 17 to evaluate the severity of this emergency.

✚ PRESCRIPTION

Matthew 28:18–20
Acts 4:31
Ephesians 4:11–12

✚ FIRST AID

A leader has to step forward.

God is absolutely going to have to do a work in the life of your church and your Sunday school. If your situation seems to be hopeless, then you are in good hands because God specializes in the impossible. He is going to work through the body of Christ. He is going to work through human instruments. Though He could have declared the Hebrews free from Egyptian bondage, you will recall that he raised up a leader, Moses, to be His spokesperson and to show the people the way.

My experience, and anything you read about Sunday school leadership, will tell you that the pastor plays a vital role. He must step up to provide hands-on leadership, or intentionally partner with a passionate leader to turn the Sunday school around. Perhaps *you* are the one that He is calling to lead your congregation from the bondage of a dying Sunday school. Who will it be? Who will step up and lead?

A decision and a declaration have to be made.

The key leaders must make an immediate decision to do whatever it takes to get the Sunday school to where it needs to be. Do not think that this is a minor point. Doing whatever it takes will mean sacrifice and will require a time commitment, flexibility, and a tenacious attitude. God has a way of stretching us when we make commitments and that can be painful because they almost always require and result in change, and this one certainly will. Ouch! However, if you do not change, you are placing your Sunday school in hospice and simply awaiting the inevitable. Do not let this happen on your watch! The key leaders, including the pastor, must make a public declaration that Sunday school is too critical to the health of the congregation to continue with a downward trend. The pastor and key leaders must declare that they are personally committed to making the necessary adjustments of time, priorities, and practices, and then call on the remaining members to do likewise.

You better get to praying.

Resurrecting the Sunday school is not a human endeavor. Leadership is provided by human instruments, but it is Jesus who is "the resurrection and the life" (John 11:25). Do not rely on your giftedness or your leadership skills. Allow God to use them, but call upon Him to work through you and commit to giving Him the glory. Moses was not a mighty man; Moses was a mighty man of God. God worked through him to do miraculous things.

Call the congregation to prayer. You could enlist twelve people for an hour each or twenty-four for half an hour each. Begin or conclude with a gathering of all members. Another option would be to gather for an hour seven nights in a row. Of course, praying should never cease, but you would do well in this case to call the congregation to prayer in a dramatic and intentional way.

Call in a specialist.

You may need an expert. That is what often happens when someone is transported to an emergency room. Once an initial diagnosis is completed by a generalist, a specialist is called upon to address the specific problem. The problem has been identified in your case. Call in someone who has experience and expertise in this particular area. It may be someone from your denomination or perhaps a leader from a church that has a thriving Sunday school. "What is it going to cost?" you may ask. Imagine a family member standing beside an ambulance and asking the paramedics that question as they work on a dying patient. The more important issue is what the cost will be of failing to address the decline. Who can you call upon for assistance?

Reestablish and refocus on the correct purpose.

The purpose of Sunday school is to study the Bible. Really? If that is the case, then why is your Sunday school dying? Bible study is central, and it is essential to the health of the Sunday school ministry, but, surprisingly, it is not the purpose. Every Sunday school would thrive if that were the case. A healthy Sunday school is focused on engaging the congregation in fulfilling the Great Commission.

Addressing the apostles, Jesus said: "All authority has been given to Me in heaven and on earth. Go therefore and make disciples of all the nations, baptizing them in the name of the Father and of the Son and of the Holy Spirit, teaching them to observe all things that I have commanded you; and lo, I am with you always, even to the end of the age" (Matt. 28:18–20). A healthy Sunday school ministry focuses on the lost being reached, lives being changed, and leaders being sent. When a congregation intentionally focuses on these aims, the result is health and growth. If any of these are neglected, the result is struggle and eventual decline. People do move and people will eventually die; therefore, failure to reach the lost will result in the decline and death of a Sunday school. The lost will not be reached if the focus is not on lives being changed. Lives are changed as God's people study and live out His word. Living it out will lead to sending and releasing leaders to serve wherever needed to accomplish kingdom tasks. What is the purpose of your Sunday school? Have you lost focus? The time has come to reestablish and refocus on the correct purpose. You will not see a change until you adjust the way you view the purpose of the Sunday school.

✛ REHAB
Establish a teacher training plan.

You will discover throughout this book the keys to having a healthy and thriving Sunday school ministry. You must understand at this point that there is not "a key." The resolutions of your problems would be a simple matter if that were the case. The challenge of Sunday school health, as is true for your personal health, is that there are several keys. What are the keys to personal health? Diet? Exercise? Relationships? Safety? Moderation? Medication? Rest? Mental health? Emotional balance? Yes! Good health is a combination of all of these, and more. Sunday school health is a balance of several practices that take a high investment of time and energy—but a high investment that has the benefit of a high return.

Something has to change. The leaders are going to need to be trained or retrained. Perhaps your leaders do not understand the dynamics of good Sunday school health, or perhaps the Sunday school has been seriously injured by some major division or change within the community to which the congregation did not adapt. Change begins with the leaders of the Sunday school.

Training will be the most common form of rehab for the issues addressed in this book. Therefore, I will endeavor to provide more specific help for you in this phase of health as you read through the other challenges. Skim ahead and note the sections on "training" to begin pulling together your plan. What is your plan for training your Sunday school leaders over the next twelve months? If they are not challenged and equipped to do otherwise, they will continue down or return to the same path.

You must increase the enrollment.

I want to give you the simplest explanation at this point. Your attendance is largely affected by your approach to Sunday school enrollment as well as the actual number of people enrolled. Let me ask you a question: Which church will have the most people in Bible study this Sunday—the church that has enrolled and is ministering to 500 people each week or the church that has enrolled and is ministering to 30 people each week? The key is not the number of people on the Sunday school roll. The key is the number of people who are receiving ministry each week from the congregation. The Sunday school roll serves as a tool to delegate the responsibility for ministry to various groups and leaders. Does your church have an expanding Sunday school enrollment? Do your leaders minister to, make contact with, and invite to fellowships those on their rolls on a regular basis? Enrolling people in your Sunday school will not in and of itself grow your ministry or keep it from dying. However, you cannot grow your Sunday school without expanding the enrollment.

You must minister through the Sunday school.

Everyone should receive ministry as they participate in Sunday school. However, long-term health will require that leaders focus on ministering to people outside of Sunday school. Contact must be maintained with people who are absent as well as those who rarely or never attend. Why? Contact must be made so that ministry needs can be identified. How will you know what the needs are if communication is not made? Once needs are identified there must be a response by the class or congregation. Have you ever been to a "loving" church? A "loving" church is one where the members are cared for and ministered to during times of need. The more people who receive care, love, and ministry during the week, the more people who show up for Bible study and worship on Sunday. Are you being intentional in this regard? Lead your groups to minister consistently to everyone assigned to their roll or group roster.

You must focus on growing leaders.

Training was mentioned previously and is one component of this task. An absence of leaders will have a major effect on the health of your Sunday school. You must get more intentional in this area to move the Sunday school forward. While I thank God for the outstanding leadership that women provide in our churches, men are critical at this point. What are you doing to grow the men in your congregation? What did Jesus do? He personally enlisted a group of men and poured His life into them. Whether it is men or women, who have you enlisted and who are you pouring your life into? Do your current teachers and leaders understand their responsibility to do likewise? Here is another point where an expert might provide some assistance. However, do not wait to get started on this critical task. Grow leaders and they will grow your groups. Lead them to grow in their faith, to grow in their skills, and to grow in their influence.

You must start new classes or groups.

You will find an entire section devoted to this based on a future question. Again, I will keep it simple at this point. Starting new classes will keep the ministry lists or the enrollment manageable for volunteer leaders. Class or group sizes will vary; however, you will need about one class for every ten attending. So if you want to average 100, you are going to need about ten classes or groups. Remember that this is a "rule of thumb" and not a "law." If you have twelve per class that will likely mean that about 25 or so are assigned to or enrolled in each group. That is a large number of people for a volunteer to keep up with, and many will not. In addition, new groups can reach out to and minister to people that the existing groups do not. Here is one example. You are not likely to have college-age young adults attending your Sunday school if there is not a class or group designated for them. They do not fit with the high school students and they do not relate to the married adults. College young adults are difficult to reach when you do have a group for them and almost impossible when you do not. Starting new groups can help you to reach out to people in life stages or affinities that existing groups do not touch. What are the plans for starting the next new class or group?

CHAPTER 2

We Are Going through a Slump

✚ THE EMERGENCY

"Slump? I ain't in no slump . . . I just ain't hitting." —*Yogi Berra*

Comedian Jeff Foxworthy is famous for explaining how "you might be a redneck if . . ." With all due respect to Mr. Foxworthy, join me as we consider how "your Sunday school may be going through a slump if . . ."

- If your parking lot is empty at 10:00 a.m. on a Sunday, your Sunday school may be going through a slump.

- If your members are claiming that daylight savings time is scheduled every Saturday night, then your Sunday school may be going through a slump.

- If your Sunday school rooms have cobwebs in them, your Sunday school may be going through a slump.

- If your children ask you, "Dad, can we go to the dentist instead?" your Sunday school may be going through a slump.

- If your church is putting want ads for Sunday school teachers in the local paper, then your Sunday school may be going through a slump.

- If your ushers are handing out pillows and blankets as members arrive, then your Sunday school may be going through a slump.

- If you have curriculum that is more than a decade old on top of the piano in a Sunday school room, then your Sunday school may be going through a slump.

- If you have members volunteering to go to the mission field so that they won't have to go to your Sunday school again, your Sunday school may be going through a slump.

- If your Sunday school teachers are excited about a film strip they are planning to show or a flannelgraph story they are going to tell, your Sunday school may be going through a slump.

- If you have more classes than you have people attending, then your Sunday school may be going through a slump.

A Sunday school going through a slump is different from a Sunday school that is dying. A church going through a slump may have strong attendance. However, the implication is that the growth has stopped or slowed. A church going through a slump has experienced growth, but the growth has come to a stop or begun to decline. What do you do when you are experiencing a slump?

✚ TRIAGE

1. Have the leaders/teachers met for training in the past two months?

2. Have there been any major holidays in the past month?

3. Is the congregation unified?

4. Has Sunday school been promoted to the congregation recently?

5. Are the members inviting guests to attend?

Diagnosis: Refer to page 17 to evaluate the severity of this emergency.

✚ PRESCRIPTION

1 Corinthians 3:6
Galatians 6:9
2 Timothy 4:5

✚ FIRST AID

Take the seasons into consideration.

Do not think it unusual to occasionally go through seasonal slumps. You may be doing many things correctly and still be affected by the various seasons. Sunday school attendance tends to go through a cycle each year.

Churches ordinarily launch new groups, reorganize, and promote children and students around August or September when school is back in session. Attendance tends to surge a bit at that point because people are home from summer vacations and the emphasis on the organizational changes and adjustments serve to elevate the Sunday school. Conversely, a holiday weekend in November followed by two holiday weekends in December will ordinarily bring a seasonal slump. Although you have a couple of great Sundays, the holiday weekends can pull the average attendance for the month down significantly. The attendance tends to bounce back once the holidays are over and as everyone resolves to do better in the new year. Once the children have their spring breaks and your members begin their summer vacations, the attendance may tend to slump again. What do you do when you encounter these seasonal slumps?

Focus on the things that you can control.

Should we cancel the holidays? Certainly not! Holidays are great for celebration, for family gatherings, and for times of respite between the ordinary routines of life. No one should be begrudged for taking time to be with family or to refresh and relax for a few days. On one hand we have a desire to maximize participation in Bible study and worship, and on the other hand we can appreciate the value of holidays and vacations.

What do you do when the attendance falls off? Remember during those seasons to focus on the things that you have control of. You may not have control of the total number of people who attend on a given Sunday. But, consider the following: Do you have control of whether you participate in or provide training? Do you have control over whether you contact and minister to those on your Sunday school roll in a given week? Do you have control over whether or not you participate in outreach? Identify a new prospect? Invest in a leader? Enroll someone else in your group? The list goes on and on. Be faithful to invest in those things that you do have control over, which in turn have an affect on the attendance. You may not see the results on the next Sunday, but you will see them in time as members return from their holiday and seasonal journeys. In addition, the slumps can be minimized if you invest in those practices that can make a difference.

Don't complain to the faithful about the unfaithful.

Understanding seasonal patterns can serve to minimize frustration when attendance falls off. People have a variety of ways that they respond to and communicate their disappointments. A word of caution is appropriate at this point. Consider these pubic statements from various Sunday school leaders or pastors:

- "I wish our members were more committed."

- "People would be here if they loved Jesus more!"

- "I don't know where everyone is today."

- "Our attendance is horrible today."

These statements may or may not be true. The problem is that you are complaining to the wrong people. It is not the fault of the people who are present that there are people who are absent. I once saw a bumper sticker that said, "The beatings will continue until morale improves!" You will find that volunteers (yes, people who attend church do so voluntarily) respond better to being challenged than being criticized. How much more true is this fact when they are being criticized for the absence of others!

Extend a challenge to your leaders and members.

Perhaps you are unsure if the slump that you are in is simply a seasonal fluctuation or the result of some deeper issue. In any case, you should never be shy about challenging your leaders or members.

Challenge your leaders when attendance is down. Challenge your leaders when attendance is steady. Challenge your leaders when attendance is up. What should you challenge them to do?

- To be faithful to worship, Bible study, and personal growth

- To be faithful to service to the body of Christ

- To be a faithful witness to those who do not know Christ

- To be faithful to minister to members of the church and community who are hurting

The body of Christ will be strengthened and attendance will grow strong if all the members are faithful to these tasks. You do not challenge your congregation by verbally beating them up. You challenge them through the teaching and preaching of God's Word; you challenge them through fervent prayer; you challenge them by modeling spiritual growth and application. Your members will be challenged through a combination of leaders verbalizing and living out the example, and the Holy Spirit working in both individual lives and the body as a whole.

Ramp up the contacts.

What is a contact? It is an intentional communication on behalf of a Sunday school class or a church that takes place during the week to minister to a member, encourage an absentee, or invite someone to attend.

Suppose that a congregation cumulatively makes fifteen contacts during the course of a week. A congregation across town that is approximately the same size makes a concerted effort to make over 200 contacts during the same week. Which congregation's attendance will be most affected the following Sunday? Consistent contacts help to minimize the effects of seasonal slumps as well to reverse a slump that may be the result of some other issue.

✚ REHAB

Spend time on evaluation.

Is the slump that you are experiencing the result of seasonal dynamics? Perhaps your attendance is slumping at a time when attendance should be up based on the patterns formerly described. How do you know? Unless it is obvious, you will need to take time to evaluate the reason for the slump. Certainly, widespread sickness in the congregation, a major holiday falling on a Sunday, a late-night community event that involved a large number of the congregation, severe weather, or some other obvious circumstance might explain the reason for the slump. But if the congregation is going through some crisis that is contentious and is either definitively or potentially the cause of division, you can be assured that is the reason for the slump.

What if the answer is not obvious and you cannot exactly identify the cause? You might consider doing one of the following:

- Bring in a person with Sunday school expertise to assist with evaluation.

- Conduct interviews with attendees, former attendees, and recent guests.

- Have leaders read and discuss a book that focuses on healthy Sunday school ministry practices.

- Grade yourself in the following areas and give attention to weaknesses identified: leader training, enrollment gain, contacts reported, outreach strategy, organization, new classes created, space utilization, leader enlistment, guest follow-up, and promotion of Sunday school as a priority ministry.

Refocus on evangelism.

Failure to focus on evangelism will lead your Sunday school from a slump to decline. The aim of growth is not to get more people from other churches to join and attend your church. Growth is a result of obedience to the Great Commission. How many people have come to trust Christ as Savior in the past couple of months? If the answer is "none," then that may be the root cause of the slump regardless of the season. Every church loses members. The loss of members is not always a negative circumstance. Over the course of time you will lose members who move out of the community, experience sickness or circumstances which prevent attendance, and, naturally, some will die. In addition, some people will waver in their commitment for a variety of reasons and some may choose to attend other churches. Failure to sow the seeds of the gospel among the unchurched will result in a decline in attendance over time, and many churches have found themselves in that circumstance. What is your evangelism strategy for the next few months? What is your plan for discipling and assimilating new believers into the life of the church?

Make sure you are encouraging your leaders.

How is the morale among your leaders? Remember that they are serving voluntarily. They will receive a reward in eternity, but a word of thanks in the present may be what is needed to get them through the week. Remember that your leaders have a great number of responsibilities related to family, work, community, and personal needs. A quality Sunday school ministry will require high standards and you'll have high expectations of your leaders. They will grow weary at times. Encouraging your leaders is the equivalent of filling the gas tank in your car. If you are not intentional about refueling, the car will run out of gas and sputter to a halt. You need to continually refuel the tanks of your leaders with expressions of appreciation, public acknowledgment of their service, prayer and ministry support, training to make them better at what they are called to do, and fellowship with other leaders. What are you doing to encourage your leaders?

Protect the unity of "the body."

Sunday school is admittedly a high-maintenance strategy, but those willing to make the investment will discover that the strategy has a high return in effective evangelism, discipleship, ministry, and assimilation of new members. Every congregation will experience occasional challenges that will test the unity of the congregation, and the manner in which these issues are addressed by the congregation will have definite affects on the ability of the congregation to reach others. A church with a poor reputation will have difficulty growing Sunday school even if all of the mechanics are being correctly applied. This doesn't mean that challenges should be ignored; however, the congregation needs to navigate through these challenges with a commitment to Christlike attitudes and a love for one another that is a testimony to the community. Protect the unity of the congregation so as not to drain energy away from the Sunday school strategy and, more importantly, as a testimony to the community of the power of Christ's love.

CHAPTER 3

Our Teachers Are Not Committed (and Often Arrive Late)

✚ THE EMERGENCY

Ladies and Gentlemen: The story you are about to hear is true. Only the names have been changed to protect the innocent. It was Sunday morning at 9:40 a.m. when I pulled into the parking lot of the Friendship Community Church. I was on this assignment with no backup, and my partner had remained at headquarters to attend to personal matters. I was on an undercover mission to investigate Friendship Church's Sunday school ministry. I was out of uniform and dressed so as to fit in with the general population. My badge and my weapons were all out of sight to give me maximum anonymity.

I immediately noted that the church had a sign near the entrance on the main highway. Several pieces of information were provided so I took note that the Sunday school would begin at 9:45 a.m. I was thankful that I was on time so as not to draw attention to myself by arriving late. Upon entering the church I was greeted by an usher who I would say was approximately six feet tall and weighed about 190 pounds with a big smile on his face. He was dressed neatly and greeted me with a friendly handshake. He thought that I was a guest attending Sunday school at his church and thus my disguise was working perfectly. He welcomed me and took me to a desk where other members were stationed to help guests find an appropriate Sunday school class. The lady at the welcome center identified an appropriate group for me and instructed the greeter to escort me there. I asked the lady, "Is this a good class?" She jokingly replied, "Do you really want to know?" "Just the facts, ma'am, just the facts," I responded. She assured me that it was.

My initial impressions were that this congregation really had their act together. However, it went downhill from there. I was ushered to a Sunday school class appropriate for my life stage. I assumed this was to maximize the probability that I could connect with people who have similar interests and experiences. We arrived at the room at exactly 9:45 a.m. I expected that several members would be present, ready to greet and welcome me, but no one was present. The greeter stated that someone would be present soon, and left me in the room all by myself. Five minutes went by. Another five minutes went by. At 9:55 a.m. the teacher finally arrived. He was friendly enough and engaged me in conversation. Members began arriving at 10:00 a.m. but no one other than the teacher engaged me in any conversation or even asked my name.

Several questions came to mind as I sat alone for ten minutes in that Sunday school room. What would I be thinking if I were not a believer? What would I be thinking if I were new in the community and looking for a new church home? How seriously do the leaders and members of this church take their faith? Do the leaders of this congregation model strong commitment?

Epilogue: Chris B. Late, Sunday school teacher at Friendship Community Church, was taken into custody. He was charged with three counts of weak commitment and one count of guest neglect. Having no prior record, he was placed on probation and at last report was serving faithfully with a renewed commitment to make a difference in his congregation and community.

✚ TRIAGE

1. Is Sunday school considered a priority ministry in your church?

2. Do you have a list of written guidelines for Sunday school leaders?

3. Does Sunday school leader training occur on a regular basis?

4. Are Sunday school teachers expected to participate in training?

5. Do your teachers typically arrive at least ten minutes prior to class?

Diagnosis: Refer to page 17 to evaluate the severity of this emergency.

✚ PRESCRIPTION

Matthew 25:14–30	Colossians 3:23
Romans 12:1–2	1 Timothy 3:1–15

✚ FIRST AID

Recommunicate purpose and priority.

Is Sunday school a priority ministry in your church? Is it clear to your leaders that it is a priority? Do your leaders understand that the purpose of Sunday school is to enable the church to fulfill the Great Commission? If you answered "no" to any of these questions, you have identified the root of the problem. For example, if your teachers believe that the purpose of Sunday school is to "study the Bible," then they can accomplish that aim even if they are fifteen or twenty minutes late. They must understand that Sunday school is more than Bible study. It is a strategy

- to reach the unchurched

- to teach God's Word

- to minister to the congregation

- to assimilate new members

Those aims cannot be accomplished by leaders with passive attitudes. Consistently arriving late, failing to communicate when absence is necessary, failing to prepare for the class, neglecting leadership apart from the Bible teaching, or resisting training all indicate that the leaders have lost sight of the purpose of Sunday school and do not understand that it is a priority ministry in your church.

Elevate and acknowledge best practices.

Do you have one or more leaders who are diligent in their commitment and responsibilities? You certainly need to express appreciation to them personally. Additionally, take an opportunity to acknowledge them publicly. The affirmation could be either verbal or written. The key is to make the affirmation so that others hear or read about it. Reward those who "go the extra mile" and exemplify good leadership. It would be awkward to call someone out for failing to show up to lead their class or for consistently being late; however, publicly expressing appreciation for someone doing a great job in some area of leadership has the dual benefit of affirming leadership and presenting a model to others of best practices. Consider the following example: Do you want your leaders to participate in training? Suppose you are going to provide six training opportunities in the coming year. Following each training session, publish—with a word of appreciation—a list of all who attended. At the conclusion of the year, in a public setting, give a certificate or some other tangible acknowledgment to those who attended four or more sessions. Give special attention to those who attended every session. Do not wait an entire year to begin doing this with other practices and expectations. Begin immediately elevating and acknowledging best practices.

Develop and communicate standards and expectations.

Here is a quick exercise. Go right now and put your hands on the document that states what time your teachers should arrive on Sunday morning. Next, find the document that states the schedule for training and the frequency of participation expected of your leaders. Finally, find the document that describes how your teachers should conduct outreach. Do you have them? If not, you have identified another reason for the lack of commitment that you are facing.

If they are not written and communicated, the standards and expectations are left to everyone's own imagination. You will find that lower standards tend to prevail if it is left to each individual to determine their own. Put together a task force of four or five teachers along with directors of Sunday school and pastoral staff. Make a list of minimum standards and expectations of Sunday school leaders. Make the list brief so as not to overwhelm your current leaders. Present these to your congregation and your teachers on behalf of the task force. Please note: No one needs to sign anything. You may be thinking that you may lose a teacher or two for even suggesting some minimum standards. Yes, that is a risk. But, please understand that if you lose them at this point it is of their own choosing and their lack of commitment has likely been detrimental to your Sunday school and would continue to be so in the future.

Back up if needed but don't back down.

You most likely will get some resistance. That is why I suggested that a task force develop the standards. An advance team allows agreement and buy-in from key leaders on the front end, keeps it from being the idea of an individual leader, and gives some momentum in advance of public presentation. Remember that if leaders step aside at this point because of the standards they do so voluntarily and have essentially admitted that they do not want to commit to doing their best in ministry.

Paul made a list of basic expectations for deacons and pastors and their wives in his letters to Timothy and Titus. Why didn't he let everyone determine the standards for themselves? Why did he communicate them in writing? Why were there certain expectations that were true for all pastors?

Low expectations are a precursor to low results. The total absence of expectations will result in a group of teachers who lack commitment to the ministry and the strategy of the Sunday school. Should you get resistance, be wise. If the push-back is extreme, you may need to back up but do not back down. In other words, make a temporary compromise if necessary, but with unapologetic communication that clearly defined standards are the direction of the future. Standards are biblical and are essential to the health of an effective Sunday school ministry. Get started on developing and communicating minimum expectations and standards.

✚ REHAB

Enlist with standards on the front end.

One of the key immediate steps to dealing with lack of commitment is to develop and communicate minimum expectations and standards. Implementation is not impossible but is challenging and will likely be accomplished only by navigating through some degree of tension. Each and every year you are likely to add one or more new teachers to lead a Sunday school group. During the course of the enlistment process, review the standards with new and prospective teachers. Be careful not to enlist leaders with the attitude that "this is easy and won't take much time." Communicate

- the priority of the Sunday school

- the purpose of the Sunday school

- the minimum expectations

Consider the result of this plan over the course of several years: As you challenge prospective leaders with the new standards and raise the bar on the front end, you can transition from a group of leaders with no clear leadership standards to a growing percentage who begin with a higher level of commitment. Supplement this approach with discussion of support systems, training opportunities, and the rewards to the congregation of having a healthy Sunday school ministry led by a group of committed teachers.

Develop a new teacher orientation plan.

Enhance and reinforce your enlistment plan with a plan for orientation of new leaders. Every teacher, from the newest rookie to the most experienced veteran, should participate the first time through. The best time to conduct orientation is three to four weeks prior to launching the new Sunday school year. The orientation should involve the senior pastor, the key leader of the Sunday school ministry, and one or two model teachers.

Prepare and provide a quality experience for your new leaders. Be sure to include discussion and instruction about the purpose of Sunday school, leadership standards, training plans, procedures, what to do when you must be absent, and available resources. Consider providing a complimentary book or other resource that will reinforce best practices for leading a Sunday school class. You might consider asking every leader to go through the orientation at least twice.

Introduce teachers to other training and models.

Some teachers have never been blessed with experiencing a healthy Sunday school model. A personal encounter with an effective Sunday school can be life-changing for those leaders and motivational to all leaders. Identify model churches within proximity of your church and take your leaders to experience their training, their ministry, and their Sunday school. Should you determine that no such model exists within a reasonable distance, identify one or more that are further away and bring some of their key leaders to train and interact with your teachers.

Connect your teachers with leaders who have higher standards and allow them to see and hear the difference that it can make. Likewise, be intentional in identifying quality Sunday school leader training in your region. Take as many teachers as possible to participate. Consider providing funding from the church budget to get as many leaders as possible to participate. Commit to go based on the value of training rather than the number of leaders willing to attend. Every leader who participates and gets the vision for a quality Sunday school ministry will strengthen your congregation and ministry.

Address uncommitted teachers.

Dealing with uncommitted teachers is a difficult task. To do so imperils relationships, raises potential conflict, and risks loss of members; however, failure to do so also bears consequences. Allowing an uncommitted teacher to continue in a leadership role places downward pressure on the standards held by all other leaders. If one teacher can stroll in fifteen minutes late every week, fail to show up on a regular basis, frequently leave prior to worship, or flirt with some questionable moral issues, how can you hold any other teacher to account for his or her level of commitment?

Do not neglect to respectfully confront ineffective teachers if you expect them to model commitment to their group members. Failure to address uncommitted teachers will keep your Sunday school from being healthy and effective. Addressing an uncommitted leader may or may not mean dismissing that person. It may be that you need to coach or purposefully invest more time with struggling leaders. You should have some established standards at this point. Those will be helpful in dealing with uncommitted teachers and will help take some of the edge off of making the issues personal. You can put everything in the context of the agreed-upon standards rather than personal judgments. Many uncommitted leaders will do you the favor of dismissing themselves as the standards are raised. As you proceed, work within the framework of the biblical process of reconciliation, local church procedures, and with the support of key church leaders.

CHAPTER 4

Our Teachers Will Not Participate in Training

✚ THE EMERGENCY

Over the years, each of my three daughters has participated in a variety of extracurricular activities, primarily centered around music and drama with a few sports activities sprinkled in between. Their musical talent is derived from their mom, and each is very gifted. Their forays into sports were partly out of curiosity and partly a way to connect with their dad's affinity for sports. Now, I appreciate culture, music, and dance as much as the next guy, and I've sat through my share of ballet performances, but if no one is getting tackled then my interest level is not piqued. By taking the girls to an occasional NASCAR race, I've ensured cultural balance in their growth and development.

Every parent can relate to the responsibilities that come with the commitment to having a child play a sport, participate in a drama production, compete on a cheerleading squad, or stay after school as a member of the chess club. The parent becomes a taxi driver, accountability partner, cheerleader, number-one fan, calendar organizer, and loan officer. (Dare I mention that the loan is never paid back?) Who knew that playing soccer, basketball, or football could cost so much? Given the investment of time and money required, the typical parent is ordinarily insistent that the coach or director has knowledge, experience, and training.

The development of children physically and socially is too important to leave in the hands of an untrained coach. Too much is at stake. Most parents would not dream of allowing their children to attend a school of untrained educators. Nor would they dare take their children to an unlicensed dentist or doctor. Why would you make a major investment for your child to be led by an untrained coach? As important as those matters are, the spiritual development of children has an even greater priority. Why would a parent dare place their child in the class of an untrained Sunday school leader? Yet staff and Sunday school directors often struggle with volunteers who do not want to participate in training. It is a bit ironic, is it not? While Sunday school teachers would agree that the study of God's Word and spiritual growth are priorities for believers, they often resist investment in their own leadership and skills to enhance their ability to be the leader needed. What do you do when your teachers are not participating in training?

✛ TRIAGE

1. Do you prepare and promote a systematic plan for teacher training each year?

2. Do you have written guidelines that state the expectations for participation in training?

3. Do you provide variety and options for your teachers to receive training?

4. Is Sunday school leader training a priority activity in your church?

5. Is the quality of the training equivalent to or better than the quality of your worship?

Diagnosis: Refer to page 17 to evaluate the severity of this emergency.

✚ PRESCRIPTION
Ephesians 4:11–12
2 Timothy 1:6
Matthew 7:24–27

✚ FIRST AID

Evaluate your current plan.
A lack of commitment on the part of your teachers can certainly be frustrating. However, you need to begin by taking an honest look at what is being offered. Is the training that is being provided worthy of their time? The triage questions can serve as a good starting point for your evaluation, but you will need to focus on a qualitative analysis at this point. Consider where you are and take immediate steps to improve in the following areas:

1. Look at the schedule. Is there a better time to provide training?

2. Look at the content. Are you helping your teachers grow in their skills?

3. Look at the format. Are you providing inspiration as well as instruction?

4. Look at the delivery. Is the right person leading training?

5. Look at the priority. Are there activities competing with the training?

6. Look at the logistics. Are you providing childcare during training?

7. Look at the promotion. Do your leaders know the topic and the time well in advance?

Evaluation is painful because you may begin to recognize that the lack of commitment is connected to the lack of quality training that has been provided. The good news is that it does not require finances to make significant improvement. Quality improvement will, however, require significant investment from a key leader. Quality improvements will not resolve the problem entirely but can enhance the degree of participation.

Survey your leaders.

You can conduct much of the evaluation yourself, and you will likely know the answers to most of the questions. However, do not assume that you know what your leaders are thinking. Seek to discover what their needs are and what adjustments might enhance their commitment to participation. A survey can take the form of personal interviews with a few key leaders, a focus group that you gather for discussion and planning, or a written survey completed by every teacher. The key is to hear the heart of your teachers and respond to their needs. Remember this key point when surveying leaders: The question is not whether training *should* be provided but how to provide training that enhances the skills of the teachers and motivates them to participate. Ask about timing, topics, quality, standards, options, and ideas for improvement. A survey will be of no value without a commitment to implement. Determine which ideas are applicable and map out a plan to incorporate the best ideas.

Get a quick victory.

Perhaps few if any leaders have participated in your training in recent months. You may have failed to offer any training recently because of declining participation. Determine to provide a quality experience that can serve to motivate your leaders. Choose a time with minimum, if any, conflicts.

I once offered a Sunday breakfast or lunch option for a church that was struggling with participation. The church had no other activities going on prior to or following services on this particular Sunday. The teachers were invited to attend a meeting over either breakfast or lunch on the designated Sunday, with the same training provided at each meal. The equipping opportunity was first introduced several weeks in advance.

In addition to a public announcement and promotion in written church materials, each teacher received a personal letter of invitation and a phone contact. The letter stated that they would get a call about two weeks in advance to determine if he or she would attend the breakfast or the lunch. Notice, the letter did not ask *if* he or she would attend but which of the two options he or she would take advantage of. The calls were made, and on the Sunday of the training every teacher was present. This took place in a church where I was told that "our teachers will not go to training." We had a great time of equipping and the attendance added to the enthusiasm. I was new in this church and we gained a quick victory.

Without a lot of comment I will add that much attention was also given to the content and the presentation for this training. The effort would have been wasted if it had flopped because of poor presentation. An appreciation banquet, a Sunday morning worship experience that incorporates equipping, or a church-hosted seminar with a prominent Sunday school speaker can likewise serve as ways to get a quick victory.

Train the trainable.

The research that I have conducted over the years has consistently shown that training is the number one determining factor in whether a church does or does not have a healthy and growing Sunday school ministry. While all leaders should be expected to participate in training, you have a responsibility to provide the training whether a large or small percentage of leaders show up. Study Ephesians 4:11–12 and you will discover that church leaders have a biblical responsibility to train the congregation in providing ministry. The implication for the congregation is that they must be willing to receive or participate in the equipping opportunities. You provide training because it is your responsibility, not because of the number of people that show up. That being said, you still should do all you can to maximize participation.

What if only a few teachers are participating? What if you can only get one or two teachers to go to that training offered by your denomination, association, or parachurch group in a neighboring community or in a retreat setting? Remember that you should not penalize those who participate because others are not participating. Provide the training. Go to the training. Train the trainable and have a great time doing it. Perhaps their experience will not only have a positive effect on their ministry but on other leaders as they hear about the experiences of those who participate.

✝ REHAB

Develop and commit to a systematic plan.

When is the next training session scheduled for your leaders? If you don't know the answer to that, then your leaders don't know either. In addition, your training is not a priority for your church or for your leaders if you cannot immediately answer this question. Each summer the pastor and key Sunday school leaders should develop a twelve-month plan that will run from August through the following July. Imagine giving your Sunday school teachers a twelve-month plan before the new Sunday school year launches. What would that accomplish? (1) You will be communicating the importance and the priority of training by working and planning in advance. (2) You will minimize conflicts by getting the dates on the church calendar and on the calendars of your leaders. (3) You will be able to maximize promotion, preparation, and the quality of the experience with additional time for planning and putting the training together.

Develop and implement a systematic plan. Should you meet every week? Some Sunday school leaders do and that is a high level of commitment. Start where you are. Plan at least four training sessions each year; strive to offer about one per month (perhaps taking a break in June and December). An annual meeting is commendable but does not account for the needs of the teachers who cannot be present. It will be a full year before they will have another training opportunity. If you have quarterly training the gap has narrowed from twelve months to three months until their next opportunity. Provide options and opportunities; do not be haphazard.

Communicate purpose and value.

Effective Sunday school leaders must grow in two areas. Failure to do so will neutralize their ability to be faithful to their call to "make disciples" as they are commanded by the Great Commission. The first area of growth is personal spiritual development. Failure to grow spiritually disqualifies a teacher from leading a Sunday school class. Spiritual growth results from the teacher's personal devotion to prayer, worship, and the study of God's Word. A teacher does not have to participate in any formal training in order to grow spiritually, but training that is done well will certainly enhance and encourage growth. The life example of the teacher is more important than any lesson the teacher will ever present to a class. Sunday school leaders are not expected to be perfect but they do have to be aware that they are modeling a relationship with Christ to those whom they lead. However, even a teacher who is growing spiritually will fail to be effective if the second area of growth is neglected. Loving Jesus is important, but that alone does not guarantee success as a Sunday school leader.

The second area of growth is skills development. What if the teacher loves Jesus but does not know how to prepare an age-appropriate Bible study? Does not know how to present the Bible study? Does not know how to motivate the members? Does not know how to lead a person to faith in Christ? Does not know how to effectively minister to the members? Does not know how to lead the class to reach out to the unchurched? Does not know how to utilize enrollment as a tool for ministry and growth? Does not know how to enlist and develop leaders? I am just getting started.

Perhaps a Sunday school teacher is a professional educator with a degree from a prominent university. Did he learn any of these skills while receiving his secular education? Not likely. Communicate to your Sunday school teachers that the purpose of training is to help them develop skills to parallel their spiritual growth, which will in turn enable them to be as effective as possible in accomplishing what God has called them to do.

Recognize and reward participation.

The task of recognition and reward is simple and an effective motivator. You are well aware that Sunday school leaders are volunteers and are not seeking monetary compensation. However, they do need acknowledgment and expressions of appreciation. You can use this to your advantage. What is the minimum that you expect of your Sunday school teachers in relation to training? Recognize those who meet those minimum standards.

Here is a simple example. Suppose you determine to provide four training opportunities and ask each teacher to read a book that you recommend and provide in the coming year to enhance their skills. First, make a public acknowledgment of all who attend a particular training session. The recognition could occur during the following worship service, or the names could be published in a newsletter or bulletin. In addition, at the conclusion of the training cycle you should do the same for all teachers who attended at least three sessions and read a book. Go the extra mile in affirming those who participated in every session.

You accomplish at least two things when you point out the participating teachers. First, you express public appreciation for their commitment. Second, although you do not call out the nonparticipating teachers, you do provide light-handed accountability as they observe others being acknowledged for participation. Take the framework of this concept and be creative and diligent in recognizing and rewarding participation in the future.

Enhance the quality of the training.

You should have received ideas from your Sunday school teachers as you conducted the survey. You probably identified several ways to improve as you took time to honestly evaluate your training. You may have noted a couple of gaps when you read through the triage section of this Sunday school emergency. You never complete the process of improving your training. What were the issues you identified? Take time to review and make a list. What improvements have you already made to enhance the quality of the training? What improvements will need to be made moving forward? Prioritize the needed improvements and set a target date for the implementation of each improvement.

Do not allow yourself to be overwhelmed. You are involved in a process. Take a step forward, but do not feel that everything has to be done at once. You will see definite results if you will be persistent, make improvements, and continue to invest in your leaders. You will begin to notice that their effectiveness increases as more and more leaders participate in training. You will be frustrated at times because some leaders fail to buy in. Don't give up. The more you invest in your leaders, the more people they will affect as they apply what they learn through the training that you plan and provide. You are truly "equipping the saints for the work of the ministry."

CHAPTER 5

We Do Not Have Any (Many) Young People

✚ THE EMERGENCY

Recipe for the slow death of a congregation:

1. Place sentimentality above purpose. Do not move, change, rearrange, renovate, or replace any existing facility where anyone has ever been saved, married, baptized, rocked as a baby, or where any donated item is present in the existing space.

2. Spend as much time as possible focusing on how great things used to be and dare not mention a vision for the future.

3. Have adult Sunday school classes do all in their power to keep their groups intact. Do not allow anyone to be recruited or send anyone to start a new class or to teach preschoolers, children, or students.

4. Assure older Sunday school members that they have "done their part" and that it is not their responsibility to staff the preschool, children's, or youth classes.

5. Do not be concerned about the quality of the music so long as no one attempts to change it.

6. Do not update any furniture or facilities. The older it looks, the better.

7. Avoid doing anything that may attract children or students to your facilities. Young people often break things, spill drinks, leave the rooms in a mess, and sometimes vandalize.

8. Do not start any new young couple's classes. Let everyone go where they are most comfortable. Allowing adults fifty years of age and up to remain in the young couple's class will help everyone to feel young.

9. Do not be concerned if the attendance is dwindling among your preschoolers, children, students, or young adults. They are just not as committed and that is not your problem.

10. Do not discern between the church's preferences and convictions. If it was good enough for our grandparents it should be good enough for our children and theirs. We should not be asked to change anything just so a few of them might trust Christ and be changed.

✚ TRIAGE

1. Have you created at least one new Sunday school class for young adults in the past five years?

2. Do you have at least five preschoolers, five children, five students, and ten young adults attending your Sunday school?

3. Does your congregation consider reaching and ministering to children, students, and young adults a priority?

4. Are you intentionally enlisting and training quality leaders to serve in your preschool, children's, youth, and young adult ministries and classes?

5. Is your congregation willing to do and try new things so long as it does not violate Scripture?

Diagnosis: Refer to page 17 to evaluate the severity of this emergency.

✚ PRESCRIPTION
Luke 18:15–16
2 Timothy 2:1–2
Psalm 78:1–8

✚ FIRST AID
Open the eyes of the congregation.

Does your congregation realize that the lack of young participants is an issue? I pointed this challenge out to a congregation that I was leading by conducting an age audit. On a particular Sunday, I had each person in every Sunday school class write one piece of information on an index card. I expressed that the information was confidential and that total honesty was needed. I asked each person to write down their age, turn the card face down, and pass it in. I followed up by getting demographic information about the population within five miles of the church location.

I was able to show the congregation that only 4 percent of

those attending Sunday school were between the ages of 20 and 39. That same group made up over 25 percent of the local population. It was an eye-opening presentation to the congregation. They did not see it until it was presented in black and white. Perhaps it is more obvious in your church. It could be that you have *no* preschoolers, children, students, or young adults. Don't wait until you are down to zero in one of these groupings to open the eyes of your congregation.

Make a decision: Live or die?

What do you do with the information once you have it? The congregation is at a crossroads whether the information was shared from an age audit or from simple observation. A congregation does not generally lose its young attendees overnight; the decline is often slow and subtle. The Sunday school is an ideal place to measure these trends because it is generally organized by age groups or life stages. A well-organized Sunday school can enable leaders to spot trends more quickly. The changes may not be as evident when looking across a larger crowd in a worship setting.

So, what if you don't have many young adults in Sunday school? The absence of young adults will naturally mean a decline of children in attendance as well as an erosion of the leadership base. A decision needs to be made. One option is to do nothing, but that is a decision to die. It will take time, perhaps ten, fifteen, or twenty years. The further the slide goes the more challenging it will be to turn it around. The worship attendance pattern will eventually follow the trend of the Sunday school. The congregation cannot wish the problem away, try to spiritualize it (*God has those here He wants here!*), or ignore it. The congregation must make a decision to live, to be healthy, to thrive, and to be obedient to the Great Commission in reaching the community. Changes will need to be made.

Listen to some students and young adults.

Some members may not like what they are about to hear, but you must engage young leaders in addressing what changes will need to be made to reach and to keep students and young adults. Church leaders need to survey students and young adults either formally or informally, but it must be done in such a way as to allow them to be completely honest. Begin by interviewing those who do attend, then interview those who have left recently, and, finally, conduct a survey of adults and students who have *never* attended your church. Consider inviting some of them to attend solely for the purpose of observing and evaluating your Sunday school ministry and worship service.

Do not discount anything that they have to share. You will likely not be able to respond to or implement every idea that is shared; however, the response and purposeful application of three, four, or five key ideas might make a major difference. The exercise may be akin to going to the doctor. He examines you and tells you things that you don't like to hear. But, you know he has your best interest at heart, so you listen and make adjustments in order to improve your health. Listen not only to what the young people say but, more importantly, to what the Holy Spirit is saying through them to your congregation.

Talk about the future and the legacy of those present.

Gather your congregation to discuss the challenge at hand. Ask them to envision what the Sunday school, the worship service, and the church as a whole will be like in a decade. What is their desire and hope for the church? Ask if it will be possible to get to where they want to go by ignoring the needs of and turning down the suggestions of students and young adults. No age group is unimportant in the life of a congregation. However, a majority of those who come to Christ and are reached by a congregation are children, students, and young adults!

If a congregation fails to reach these groups, the result is ultimate decline. Do the current members desire for the church to be thriving ten, twenty, and fifty years from the present? The decisions made today will affect the health of the church in the future. God forbid that decisions made by today's members would result in the ultimate death of the congregation. It does not have to happen, and it is not the will of God. Talk about the future and agree that God wants your church to be healthy and to make a difference in the community for generations to come.

All hands are required on deck.

Are the members serious about turning the tide and strengthening the participation of preschoolers, children, students, and young adults? A commitment of several years may be required. A "whatever it takes" attitude is critical on the part of the current members. It will require current members to lead Sunday school classes rather than sitting in them. The church must staff classes or small groups for all ages, regardless of the number of attendees in a given class.

Perhaps members are thinking that the congregation does not need a preschool teacher because there are no preschoolers attending. That mind-set has to change. Could it be that no preschoolers are present because there is no one prepared for them if they attend?

Suppose that you now have a room, a teacher for the class, and all of the training and materials needed. But you still don't have any students. Now what? You have to be aggressive. The leader of the class has to be assertive in identifying, reaching out to, enlisting, providing activities for, and inviting people to attend. He or she will have to invest time apart from Sunday morning. Guests and prospective members will not just show up. In addition, the congregation must get more assertive in ministering to and identifying people in the age groupings where the gaps were discovered. To turn around the Sunday school in this circumstance will require that all hands are on deck.

✚ REHAB

Accept that gains may result in losses.

What changes will have to be made? That will vary from congregation to congregation. Leaders should never sacrifice biblical convictions or violate Scripture to accomplish any task. However, congregations and individual members are prone to have preferences, traditions, sentiments, and an occasional sacred cow that is deeply entrenched in their church culture. These are not necessarily biblical concepts—although many people are skilled at making a loose connection in order to maintain their own deeply held preference. Failure to reach young people will result in the demise, decline, and ultimate death of the congregation.

Do you hang on to the preferences to maintain a level of comfort in the present while sacrificing the future life of the congregation? Or do you sacrifice current levels of comfort to preserve the future life of the congregation? If you choose the latter, you will hurt some feelings. As a matter of fact, you may lose a family, or even several. What I'm describing is not a simple issue. Prayer and wisdom are essential in navigating these challenges. However, leaders must come to terms with the reality that desired long-term gains may result in the loss of some good and well-meaning members. Losing them is not the goal, but it may be a difficult reality. May God grant wisdom and may the losses be minimal as you proceed.

Staff according to priorities.

At this point I'm referring primarily to volunteer staff, although the application could be made to ministerial staff as well. I find that congregations are great at starting ministries but often struggle with stopping ministries. Often a church that has decreased in attendance continues to attempt to provide the same level or number of ministries that were provided when attendance was much higher. The result is that the remaining leaders are often stretched between several ministry responsibilities. Some good ministries may need to be put on hold, suspended, or even eliminated. Remember that *none* of the ministries will exist in a few years if students and young adults are not reached. Staffing the Sunday school and ministries to preschoolers, children, students, and young adults is critical at this point. None will flourish in the absence of leadership. Unless a ministry is essential—meaning that the church cannot function without it—consider suspending it in order to give remaining leaders total focus on reaching young people. If the church will do so, the result will be a growth in the leadership base, which will enable ministries to revive in the future.

Strive for CQI (Continuous Quality Improvement).

You may have noticed that there has been no specific discussion of style. Does a church need to be contemporary in order to reach young adults? I am blessed to work with hundreds of churches each year and can honestly show you traditional churches, contemporary churches, and everything in between that are reaching all ages. I can also show you churches of every style that are in decline. I have my own preferences and biases about style, and that is likely true of you also.

One observation that I have made as I work with churches is that it doesn't matter what your style is if you do it poorly. By way of example, I'm often asked if a congregation should dismantle the Sunday school in favor of weekday small groups. Please note that I am an advocate of both and an opponent of neither. Here is the challenge: If the congregation does not do Sunday school well, then what makes them think they will do small groups well? If they can honestly say that they are doing it correctly, with quality and with total commitment and it is not working, then perhaps they need to consider alternatives. I rarely find this to be the case. Typically, the Sunday school is being poorly led, it is not a priority, and no adjustments have been made.

Quality does not mean *perfection*. Quality implies that something is being done well and that continual effort is made to improve. Why would anyone want to participate in anything that is poorly applied? Is Sunday school being done well in your church? How about your worship service? How about the childcare provided during your worship service? Take time to evaluate the quality of your ministry and continually seek to make improvements. It may be that you need to make some adjustments in style. That may or may not mean major changes; even small adjustments can make a big difference. Go back to what you learned from your survey of students and young adults to discover how great this need is. "And whatever you do, do it heartily, as unto the Lord and not to men" (Col. 3:23).

Improving quality is not intended as a way to improve on the working of the Holy Spirit. That wouldn't even be possible and it is not the intention. The goal is to remove anything that might distract someone from being attentive to the work of the Spirit. You can be thankful that the Holy Spirit works in spite of your flaws. Seek to improve quality of ministry out of gratitude for Christ's work and pray that the Holy Spirit will guide and work through you as you seek to give your best to Him.

Call in "missionaries."

You have a need, and If the decline has been steep, you may require missionary assistance. Perhaps your Sunday school is absolutely depleted of young people. If you are down to a few aging members and leadership is sorely lacking, you should certainly contact your denomination or local association of churches for assistance. The sooner you do this, the more likely they can assist. Use Matthew 9:37–38 as a template for prayer in your congregation. Ask God to send you leaders, and commit that you will henceforth be a sending congregation.

Consider contacting ten or more churches within your geographic area—churches that share your values and biblical convictions. Make a personal and direct request that they send a leader, couple, or family to serve as missionaries in your church for twelve to twenty-four months. Contact multiple churches asking for one leader (or family) rather than one church asking for multiple leaders. Rick Warren, pastor of Saddleback Church in California, says that the "health of a church is measured more by its sending capacity than its seating capacity." Every missionary who goes overseas leaves from an established congregation. The planting of a church typically involves the release of members from a local congregation to assist with the new congregation. Perhaps you are in a healthy church. Are you sending missionaries? Releasing members is a compliment to the health of your church and a direct application of obedience to the Great Commission To receive or release members for a season of investment in a struggling church is a great example of being kingdom-minded. Seek missionaries now and commit to send them as God blesses your church.

Take advantage of the fertile soil.

Remember that most people trust Christ as Lord and Savior during or prior to their teen years. How assertive is your congregation in reaching out to and sharing the gospel with children and students? The top evangelistic churches in our state report that vacation Bible school is still one of their most effective evangelistic ministries. The Great Commission begins with the admonition to "go." Are you waiting on and wishing for children, students, and young adults to come to your church, or is your congregation "going," purposefully sharing the gospel and seeking to reach them? They are the group that is most open to the gospel and yet many declining Sunday school ministries and congregations are doing little or nothing to reach them with the good news of the gospel. Develop a plan to take advantage of the fertile soil by increasing the amount of sowing done by your congregation.

CHAPTER 6

We Do Not Have Enough Leaders

✛ THE EMERGENCY

Ricardo had been serving as Sunday school director at Second Community Church for only a few months. He was slowly learning the basic administrative tasks required of his leadership role and was starting to apply many of the principles he had learned from reading a couple of books on Sunday school growth. He was beginning to discover that the Sunday school had many moving parts and that a long-term commitment would be required to make a real difference.

One of the challenges that he faced early on was to secure enough teachers to lead the classes. Much of this process was left to him, in spite of the fact that the church had a nominating team responsible for identifying and enlisting ministry leaders. Although he had enthusiastically accepted the opportunity to serve in the role of Sunday school director, he was soon disappointed by the lack of willingness of members to make commitments to serve. He reluctantly combined a couple of classes in order to get the new Sunday school year launched.

Within only a few weeks of serving in his new role, Ricardo faced an enlistment crisis. A key church family would be moving within two weeks due to an immediate job transfer. Both the husband and the wife taught Sunday school classes and had to resign with only a week's notice. The wife taught one of the two preschool classes and the husband taught an adult class. Filling the roles for a week or two would not be too much of a challenge. Ricardo had no idea how difficult it would be to enlist new leaders to fill the vacant positions.

The pastor graciously announced the need from the pulpit for a couple of Sundays and a notice was placed in the church bulletin for a month. Unfortunately, no one responded to these public appeals. Ricardo decided to take a more direct approach. Obviously, all of the prospective leaders were those attending adult classes, so Ricardo went to the teachers of those classes. Ricardo was shocked when one of the adult teachers told him to "leave my class alone." His class had a "great fellowship" and he "did not want it disrupted." Ricardo was even more assertive with the next adult Sunday school teacher, and specifically asked if he would enlist someone from his class to fill the preschool leader role. That teacher's reluctance was similar, and yet Ricardo pressed: "How about the Mannings? They would be great in preschool!" The teacher responded: "Don't take the Mannings. They are my best members." Ricardo responded in frustration: "Well then, who are your worst members? Perhaps we could put them with the preschoolers!"

Ricardo was both disappointed and frustrated. Among several dozen adults, no one would make a commitment to minister to these precious children. How would the Sunday school ever thrive if the adult classes failed to produce leaders?

✛ TRIAGE

1. Do you have a systematic plan for training Sunday school teachers?

2. Do your adult Sunday school teachers understand their role in developing and sending forth leaders to serve in other areas?

3. Is there an emphasis on teachers of all age groups taking responsibility for personally enlisting and developing an apprentice teacher?

4. Does your church have an ongoing enlistment plan throughout the year?

5. Do you prioritize one-on-one enlistment over enlistment by public announcement?

Diagnosis: Refer to page 17 to evaluate the severity of this emergency.

✚ PRESCRIPTION
Ephesians 4:15b–16
Luke 6:12–16
Acts 6:1–7
Matthew 9:37–38

✚ FIRST AID
Buy time by appealing for interim commitments.

What does a congregation do when they lose a pastor? They often call an interim pastor to serve for a few weeks or months while the congregation seeks a permanent replacement. The procedure for this circumstance varies by denomination, but the concept can be easily understood regardless of your church custom. It would not usually be wise for a church to call as their new pastor the first person who comes to their attention. Because this decision is vital to the future of the church, the leaders must screen candidates with due diligence.

The same principle can be applied for Sunday school

leadership. When a teacher or other leader resigns, it is sometimes difficult to quickly find someone willing to make a long-
term commitment. (It will be particularly challenging if your
church has failed to previously develop and implement a comprehensive enlistment plan.) You will find it easier to enlist a
replacement for four to six weeks than for several months. The
interim replacement may even discover that the leadership role
he is filling is something God is calling him to on a long-term
basis. If not, you have bought time to seek out long-term replacement. At the end of six weeks, you may find that you need
to replace the interim with another interim, though the aim is
to fill the role as soon as possible with a leader committed for
the balance of the year, and hopefully beyond.

Transition from public appeal to direct enlistment.

The most common form of enlistment is also the least effective. Imagine this scenario: A teacher needs assistance with
outreach and announces to her class that she needs an outreach
leader. As soon as class concludes, several people respond,
asking to be awarded the outreach role.

Is that how it happens? No! Rather, every member assumes
the teacher is referring to someone else when she makes an appeal for an outreach leader.

How often have you seen or heard an appeal for teachers
or leaders from the pulpit or in a church bulletin or newsletter
for several weeks? It's no sin to make such an announcement.
You may occasionally be blessed to find the help needed in
this manner, and it can be used to supplement your enlistment
strategy in some circumstances. But it should *supplement* your
strategy rather than be the *key* strategy for your enlistment.
One potential negative consequence of public appeal is that
someone may volunteer who is unqualified and could do more
harm than good if placed in the vacant role.

Follow the model that Jesus presented when enlisting the

apostles. You will note in Luke 6:12–16 that He prayed about whom He should call and went to them directly and asked them to serve. If you need a new Sunday school leader, pray and discuss who God is leading you to invite to serve in the vacant role. Elevate both the importance of the leadership role and the value of the person you are asking by meeting with him or her personally in order to communicate the vision, the support, and the opportunity for the vacant role. Ask them to pray and seek God's guidance. The Holy Spirit plays a critical role in the process of calling a person to a new area of ministry. God will work whether the individual accepts, rejects, or perhaps offers to assist in some other way. Most people are far more responsive to a direct request or challenge than to a generic appeal from the pulpit or some written announcement.

Meet with adult Sunday school teachers.

You have probably had meetings in your home when there is an issue that needs to be honestly placed on the table. If Mom or Dad turn off the television and gather the entire family to discuss a matter, the subject must be of importance and a response must be expected.

Call your teachers who lead adult classes for a "family meeting." Following a time of brief fellowship and prayer, introduce the following line of reasoning: Sunday schools are generally divided into preschool classes, children's classes, youth classes, and adult classes. Where do the preschool leaders come from? (Everyone should be aware that preschoolers cannot teach preschoolers. All preschool leaders must come from adult Sunday school classes.) Where do children's leaders come from? How about youth Sunday school teachers? What if a new teacher is needed for an adult class?

Do you see a pattern here? Each and every current leader must come from adult Sunday school classes. Future leaders reside in the preschool, children's, and youth classes, of course, but current leaders reside in the adult classes. What does that mean? It means that if adult Sunday school leaders are not intentional about developing and sending out leaders, the preschool, children's, and youth classes will struggle and fail. Is that the desire of any current leader? Take your adult leaders on a journey with Jesus and the apostles. Notice how He enlisted them, helped them in their spiritual development, equipped them, and ultimately sent them out. Ask your adult Sunday school leaders to adopt the same approach with their members. They must be willing to release members to serve in other areas. The future of the congregation depends on it!

✚ REHAB
Establish a training plan for current teachers.

At this point, let us consider why training is essential to enlistment rather than how to conduct the training. You have already discovered that direct enlistment is critical and that adult Sunday school leaders must be intentional in releasing members. How is that going to happen? One of the positive consequences of developing a twelve-month equipping plan where teachers are expected to gather several times a year is the leadership growth that will be experienced by many teachers. You will likely have some teachers who falter or resist commitment to training. However, consider what happens in the lives of those who are participating. Suppose that four or five of your teachers are participating in training on a regular basis. Imagine that on a scale of 1 to 10 their leadership skill level is about a 3. Bear in mind that they love the Lord and are committed to the church, but their leadership is nominal at best.

Suppose that the skills they develop over the next few months raise their leadership ability from a 3 to a 5. You will find that as their skills increase, their improved leadership will influence those whom they regularly gather with. You are not likely to find members who have greater levels of leadership skills than those who lead them. A member with a leadership skill level of 7 would not feel challenged in a church such as we are describing, and would likely seek another congregation. Here is where the dots begin to connect. As the leadership skills of the teachers grow, the leadership potential of their followers grow. Then, when it comes time for enlistment, it is much easier to find capable leaders among those who are at higher levels of leadership ability. Failure to provide training for your teachers is a barrier to effective enlistment.

Challenge all teachers to enlist an apprentice.

Enlisting one person is much easier than enlisting a dozen leaders. What if every current teacher would take responsibility for enlisting and equipping one new leader in the next year? Consider how future enlistment would be affected.

Suppose that the challenge to enlist an apprentice teacher is extended at the beginning of the Sunday school year to a church with ten classes or groups. Eight of the ten teachers honestly try to meet the challenge. Suppose that five of those eight succeed and begin mentoring a prospective new teacher. Perhaps it turns out that one of the apprentice teachers has no skills or gifts in the area of teaching. No problem. Better to find that out in this environment than after placing him or her in a group and having it flop. You will have to consider whether the apprentice can develop the necessary skills over a longer period of time or if the individual needs to be guided in a different direction.

This scenario leaves the church with four apprentice teachers in ten groups. As the new Sunday school year is approaching, you discover that two teachers will not be returning to their roles and the church needs to start one new class. That means you will need three new teachers. Here is a dilemma that your Sunday school may have never faced before: You have three teaching vacancies and four people who are seeking a place to teach! Is that the way it will happen in every situation? Certainly not! No individual principle is proposed to serve as the total solution. However, you can stay a step ahead of enlistment by emphasizing apprentice teachers.

Develop a year-round enlistment strategy.

It is common to focus on enlistment during a narrow time frame of a few short weeks when there is a push to staff the new Sunday school year. Instead, develop a year-round enlistment strategy that includes a comprehensive equipping plan, an emphasis on all teachers enlisting an apprentice, and an understanding among adult Sunday school leaders of their critical role in sending forth leaders.

These ideas can further enhance your enlistment process throughout the year:

1. Ask the nominating team or committee to serve throughout the year seeking to identify and enlist leaders as far in advance as possible rather than waiting until a few weeks prior to a new cycle.

2. Allow age group directors or staff to enlist teachers for their ministries directly. You will find that teachers are more responsive to the leadership of a person who enlisted them rather than to someone to whom they were assigned.

3. Train teachers and emphasize individual class organization. Encouraging members to serve in individual groups will ordinarily help the classes to be more effective with increased participation. Then, you will find it easier to enlist from those who are already serving in smaller commitment roles, such as those with group

responsibilities, compared to those who sit in a class with no responsibility.

4. Train all leaders, including Sunday school teachers, on how to enlist directly.

5. Offer a potential new teacher training course once or twice each year.

Be sure that you are not spreading leadership resources too thin.

Remember that you cannot expect fifteen adult volunteers to fill one hundred ministry roles. Sometimes enlistment difficulty stems from asking too much from too few. I believe that everyone should serve, but I understand that it's not likely.

How many adults attend your Sunday school? Multiply that number by .80. Keep the total you just calculated in mind. Now, how many leaders does it take to staff all Sunday school leader roles, fulfill choir or music ministry roles, serve on all committees/teams, staff Sunday evening and Wednesday evening ministry offerings, and lead recreational and ministry commitments throughout the week? How does that number compare with the number of adults available to serve per your previous calculation? Do you have greater leadership needs or greater leadership availability? It may be time to reevaluate, suspend some ministry offerings, and prioritize. Please understand that failure to provide quality leadership for your Sunday school will result in a further erosion of your leadership base. Don't spread your Sunday school teachers or your church leaders too thin.

CHAPTER 7

A Lot of People on Our Rolls Do Not Attend

✚ THE EMERGENCY

Jesus shared an inspiring and challenging parable in Luke 15:3–7 (HCSB):

> So He told them this parable: "What man among you, who has 100 sheep and loses one of them, does not leave the 99 in the open field and go after the lost one until he finds it? When he has found it, he joyfully puts it on his shoulders, and coming home, he calls his friends and neighbors together, saying to them, 'Rejoice with me because I have found my lost sheep!' I tell you, in the same way, there will be more joy in heaven over one sinner who repents than over 99 righteous people who don't need repentance."

He follows in Luke 19:10 by pointing out: "For the Son of Man has come to seek and save the lost" (Luke 19:10 HCSB).

Sunday school leaders are well-meaning when they desire that everyone attend every Sunday. The reality is that people are absent each week for a variety of reasons, including sickness, emergencies, travel, and, yes, sometimes because of a lack of commitment. Many fail to attend altogether, and that is so frustrating to those who are committed. Have you ever wondered how the passages in Luke 15:3–7 and Luke 19:10 might read if today's leaders wrote them in the context of their frustration? Here are some possibilities:

> "What man among you, who has 100 sheep and loses one of them, does not *remind himself that 99 out of 100 is better than average and does not concern himself with the one that is lost, but with the 99 that are present. And he says to his neighbors and friends, 'Rejoice with me for 99 places us at the front of most other flocks. For the Son of Man came to serve those who are faithful.'*

Or the parable might read like this:

> "What man among you, who has 100 sheep and loses one of them, does not *after several weeks shear him from the roll? And when he has removed him improves his percentages and is able to give more attention to the faithful. And he says to his neighbors and friends, 'Rejoice with me because we are now at 100% (99 out of 99). For the Son of Man came to keep the percentages up!'*

Here is one more possibility:

> "What man among you, who has 100 sheep and loses one of them, does not *send an e-mail or make a call seeking a reply. But,*

when none is given shakes the dust off of his feet recognizing that time and energy are limited and cannot be wasted on someone who does not immediately respond. And he says to his neighbors and friends, 'Rejoice with me for I have done my part.' For the Son of Man came so that I would make good use of my time!"

Are you frustrated because there are many people on the rolls who are not attending? Your frustration is not the problem. You should desire for people to be committed to Christ. However, don't let your response to this issue add to the problem. What should you do when you have a lot of people on your rolls who are not attending?

✚ TRIAGE

1. Do 45 percent or more of those enrolled attend on a typical Sunday?

2. Do your leaders report the number of contacts made each week when turning in records?

3. Does everyone enrolled in a group get a personal contact on a regular basis?

4. Do your leaders intentionally establish a relationship with everyone on the class roll?

5. Do your leaders view their Sunday school rolls as ministry lists rather than attendance lists?

Diagnosis: Refer to page 17 to evaluate the severity of this emergency.

✚ PRESCRIPTION

Luke 15:3–6   John 15:12–17
1 Corinthians 12:18   Ephesians 4:11–16

✚ FIRST AID
Resist the urge to purge (but conduct an honest audit).

What do you do when you have large numbers of people on the Sunday school rolls that rarely or never attend? Churches often elect to "purge the rolls" by deleting anyone and everyone who has not attended in the previous year. "Why must I keep them on my roll?" a teacher will ask. "They never attend." Consider the following before making a decision to "purge" your rolls.

First, enrollment is not the same as church membership. A person does not have to be a member of the church to be on a Sunday school roll. A person enrolled is one to whom the Sunday school class or small group is committed to minister. A church member is someone who has made a commitment to the local church. You may argue that persons who no longer attends should be removed from membership since they are not keeping their commitment. You may have a point, and your congregation can wrestle with that question. However, I would urge you to keep them on the Sunday school roll so long as you can provide ministry.

Second, it is appropriate to "audit" your Sunday school rolls, and this can be done without "purging" them. You should do this each week (or at least regularly) as each group maintains contact with all of those enrolled. If a person has died or moved to another state, by all means remove his or her name because of your inability to continue to minister to that person. "Purging" occurs when you remove names in mass because of their lack of attendance without regard to the class's frequency of contact and ministry. Do not penalize members of the community or your congregation by removing them and ceasing ministry because of a group's failure to keep their commitment to maintain contact and ministry.

Third, you cannot increase the attendance while decreasing the enrollment. Like you, I want everyone to be present every week. However, each week you will have people who are out of town, sick, dealing with emergencies, working, or struggling with their spiritual commitment. You will not average 100 percent attendance, and that is not the aim of your Sunday school enrollment. The aim is to regularly minister to 100 percent of those enrolled, and if your church will do so while continuing to add others to the ministry lists (rolls), you are much more likely to experience growth than if you purge the rolls and minister to fewer people.

Audit? Absolutely. Purge? Big mistake! Maintain contact and ministry? That's the real key to a healthy Sunday school or small group ministry!

Check the elevation.

Is it possible that the pastor or congregation places a much higher priority on worship than on the small group experience? Even the healthiest congregation will ordinarily have more people attending worship than small groups or Sunday school. Most of the gap that the church is experiencing between the number attending and the number enrolled is likely a combination of deficiencies in the Sunday school ministry combined with a lack of emphasis on Sunday school involvement by key leaders.

Ideally, everyone enrolled in a class is in attendance, but that is not necessary to have a healthy Sunday school. Some members will be absent for specific reasons. In addition, you will have members with varying levels of maturity and commitment. Do we "kick out" those who are less mature? Do we cease to reach out to those who have been out of town? An average attendance of 40 to 60 percent is typical for most Sunday school ministries. (These figures are based on annual church profiles from Georgia and my work with hundreds of churches.) You can keep the percentages up by removing those who do not attend, but you will likely decline in average attendance over time if you do so. Remember that you cannot average more by ministering to fewer.

A failure to emphasize and elevate the Sunday school as a key ministry in your church will only exacerbate the situation. Your congregation must know that Sunday school is not an add-on, not a program, and not an additional activity, but rather a key strategy for your church to reach the lost, lead members to grow, develop leaders, and minister to the congregation. Those enrolled are the ones receiving most of the ministry and providing nearly all of the leadership. Does your congregation recognize this truth? Does the pastor elevate the Sunday school as a key ministry in the church and urge the involvement of all? If not, the gap in attendance and enrollment will continue to be an issue.

Conduct the "contact crazy" experiment.

How many contacts were reported by those involved in your Sunday school ministry in the past week? A contact is an intentional communication on behalf of the Sunday school class through phone call, text, e-mail, social networking, personal visits, cards, or purposeful conversation when you encounter people in your community. If few people were contacted in a given week, you will ordinarily observe that fewer of those enrolled are present the following Sunday. If contacts are not reported, you can only guess at how many were actually made. Contacts are a tool to keep the members connected, to invite those who have never attended, to discover ministry needs and opportunities for those who are hurting, and to encourage those who have recently been absent.

Is it possible that a large number of those enrolled have not received any contact in recent weeks or months? Is it possible that some of your groups have not invited any guests to attend recently? The reason for the lack of contacts can be rooted in lack of training, misunderstanding of purpose, weak teaching or class dynamics that affect desire to make contacts, or a combination of these factors. However, failure to invite, call absentees, and to minister to everyone enrolled will have a negative effect on attendance even if the teaching and class dynamics are strong.

Select a target week within the next month and extend a challenge to your leaders. You can give a special name or emphasis to the Sunday that is chosen if you wish. Ask everyone to be prepared and to expect attendance to be higher. Ask your leaders to work with group members to make a personal phone call or send a letter or email to every person on the Sunday school roll; have every class invite as many people as possible; and make contact with any prospects. In short, make as many contacts as possible. You can place a challenge before your leaders, such as a goal for total contacts of three times the number of people enrolled. The key is to put together a plan, promote it, and lead as many members as possible to participate. A higher than normal number of contacts will ordinarily result in more people in attendance. You will need to follow up by helping your leaders make the connection between the higher attendance on the special day and the number of contacts that were made. Follow through by emphasizing and measuring contacts on a systematic basis.

Reestablish the role of the roll.

Everyone on the Sunday school roll (or small group roster) is a person whom the class or group has made a commitment to minister. The best practice for utilizing enrollment to maximize effectiveness in outreach, ministry, fellowship, and personal growth is to view the lists as "ministry lists" and not "attendance lists." The criteria for being on a Sunday school roll is not frequency of attendance but the ability of the class to minister to the individual. That is not to suggest that you should not desire for them to attend regularly.

Add someone to the roll at the point you can begin ministry and remove someone from the roll when ministry can no longer occur. If my daughter attended your church and later dropped out, at what point would I want you to stop ministering to her? *Never.* Once you remove her from the roll and stop interacting with her, you are practically guaranteeing that she will not reconnect with your congregation. Leave her on the roll so long as you can minister to her in spite of your frustration that she is not attending. Here is the key: You must continue to actively minister to her!

How do your leaders view their rolls? Do they take a copy home each week to make contacts, to call absentees, and to discover ministry needs? Failure to do so on the part of the leaders will guarantee a low percentage of those enrolled in attendance each week. The leader of the class or group is responsible for personally knowing everyone on his or her roll and organizing the class to ensure that every one of them receives regular contact regardless of frequency of attendance. Regular contact serves not only in the discovery of ministry needs and keeping members connected but also as an ongoing audit. Regular contact will lead to immediate discovery if someone has joined another congregation or moved out of the community. Train your teachers to utilize the roll as a tool to keep connected and to minister to all of the members.

✛ REHAB
Get your leaders back on the train.
Are you meeting with your leaders on a regular basis? When is the last time that you discussed the role of the roll, contact practices and methods, healthy class dynamics, relationship development, teaching methods, or how to discover and follow up prospects? The subjects included in the preceding question are not exhaustive. Any and all of these issues can affect the number of those who are enrolled that are attending as well as

the potential for growth. You will find that your Sunday school leaders will do what they are taught, led, and motivated to do. Are you teaching them?

Most Sunday school teachers focus primarily on teaching and aren't aware that more is required in leading a healthy class. Even Sunday school teachers with degrees in education will not have learned the dynamics that lead to good attendance or growth in attendance. The skills needed to lead a healthy Sunday school must be taught by someone. Who is doing it? And you must re-teach the skills. Suppose you spend a training session discussing how to best utilize Sunday school rolls. You will have to teach it again next year. Why? Because some of your leaders were likely absent when you taught it. Some leaders may not have "gotten it" or may have reverted to old habits and need to be challenged again. Plus, new leaders will have come on board. You will have to get your leaders involved in ongoing training if you desire for more of those on your rolls to be in attendance each week.

Emphasize and track contacts.

One of the short-term steps discussed in the first-aid section was to conduct a "contact crazy" experiment. Now is the time to take the long view. One of the best ways to emphasize contacts is to track them. Simply ask each class to report the total number of contacts made by the group each week. The task requires only a few seconds on the part of the teachers or class administrators each week. They should ask class members to share the total number of contacts made in the past week by passing around a report sheet or having them hold up the number of fingers equivalent to contacts made.

You will quickly learn which groups are ministering to their members and inviting guests. Suppose that the following number of contacts are reported by a group over the next eight weeks: 0, 0, 0, 3, 0, 1, 0, 0. What can you conclude from that information? You can likely conclude that little ministry is occurring and that no one is being invited. No wonder they are struggling with attendance. Consider the total contacts of another group: 17, 11, 2, 22, 11, 4, 12, 18. Do you suppose this group may be doing more ministry and inviting more guests?

Also track the cumulative number of contacts for the entire Sunday school ministry. Over the course of time, you should be able to see observable patterns between contacts and attendance. You will also be able to identify groups that are struggling, and when you notice reductions in contacts that will prompt you to give renewed emphasis to this key strategy.

Help your leaders apply the two-pronged magnet (teaching and relationships).

A magnet is a tool of attraction. Your Sunday school leaders have a great motivation for attracting both members and guests to attend their Bible study. Your members need the interaction, accountability, connection, and ersonal growth that can occur in being part of a small group of believers. Guests can hear the gospel, receive ministry, and develop meaningful relationships when they are invited and attend a small group. What is it that keeps members connected and attracts guests?

Your leaders have a two-pronged magnet that can be utilized more effectively when both prongs are engaged. Good teaching along with strong class dynamics are important and represent the first prong of the magnet. The teaching and the class do not have to be perfect, but there are some minimums:

- Members and guests should be warmly received when they arrive.

- Interaction should take place through fellowship and sharing of prayer and ministry needs.

- The teacher should share an age-appropriate, well-prepared Bible study.

- The Bible study should include interaction with opportunities to discuss and ask questions.

- The study should be Bible-centered and include personal application.

- The group should fellowship, minister, and do outreach together regularly.

- Teaching cannot be dry, lifeless, or passionless.

With good teaching skills, a dynamic teacher can attract many members and guests. The strong teaching may even provide some degree of motivation for members to invite others. However, no one new will likely attend if they are not invited. Those who have fallen away will not return if the class does not express personal concern.

The second prong of the magnet is relationships. Relationships do not develop simply because Bible teaching is taking place. The group members must interact while they are together. You should not gather without spending time teaching the Word of God, nor should you feel reluctance to allow time for fellowship when you meet together. Enhance the fellowship by planning time together in addition to the gathering for Bible study. Relationships will be further enhanced as you discover and respond to ministry needs of the class members. Combining excellent teaching with refreshing relationships will keep members connected and the number of those enrolled attending at a much stronger level.

CHAPTER 8

Our Worship Attendance Is Much Larger Than Our Sunday School Attendance

✚ THE EMERGENCY

Where did they go? Eight years ago Crossroads Community Church was struggling. The church had been planted about forty years earlier and steadily grew for about twenty-five of those years. The membership reached nearly 400 and it was not unusual for over 200 people to attend the Sunday morning worship. Unfortunately, the pastor had some problems that negatively affected the church. Following his resignation the attendance dropped to well below 100 practically overnight. Many people were hurt and guests were almost nonexistent as the stories were discussed throughout the community.

The next seven years were quite a struggle. Three different pastors came and went during that time, and the church would have floundered were it not for the strong commitment of five or six key families. That is when Crossroads Church was blessed to call Pastor Jameson. He was younger than the previous pastors but was outgoing, energetic, and as likeable as anyone you would ever meet. Though he had served as pastor in only one congregation prior to Crossroads, it was obvious that he had learned and grown much from the experience.

The first year of Pastor Jameson's ministry was unbelievable. His energy and dynamic preaching ability seemed to quickly erase the struggles of the previous seven years. He personally invited guests, reached people for Christ, and served as a model for engaging the unchurched in the community. The members quickly caught on and started enthusiastically inviting friends and neighbors. Worship grew dramatically from around 50 to over 150 within a year. The church grew to over 250 the next year and was exploding with new members. The good news is that many people were coming into a relationship with Jesus Christ. The worship service was exciting and served as the highlight of the week for so many. Though the growth slowed, it did continue and reached above 400 within a few years. The growth brought challenges, but they were overcome by God's grace and with the leadership of Pastor Jameson and key members.

The Sunday school grew somewhat on the wave of the worship growth but was never a priority for Pastor Jameson. He was satisfied so long as members came to worship and the growth continued. Sunday school attendance had grown but was less than one-fourth of the worship attendance. The church was stunned the morning that Pastor Jameson read his letter of resignation. His reputation had grown along with his skills, and a church almost twice the size of Crossroads offered a great opportunity for ministry in a neighboring state. The resignation and transition were all done with great integrity and Pastor Jameson was certainly to be missed. Most of the congregation had come to know Christ as Savior under Pastor Jameson's ministry.

Once Pastor Jameson left, the worship attendance dropped immediately and dramatically. Attendance was down by over 100 within a month of his departure and seemed to still be bleeding after three months. The church called an interim pastor, and he was a fine preacher, but attendance continued to decline. Where did everyone go? The connection point at Crossroads for a majority of the members had been severed. The Sunday school never grew much above 100 while Pastor Jameson was there. However, it was interesting that while the worship attendance had declined dramatically, the attendance in Sunday school had barely dropped at all since he left.

✚ TRIAGE

1. Is the quality of your Sunday school ministry equivalent to the quality of the Sunday morning worship service?

2. Does the pastor frequently emphasize the value and importance of involvement in Sunday school?

3. Does the church emphasize the value of Sunday school for all age groups?

4. Does your church seek to assign or enroll all of your resident members into a Sunday school class?

5. Do at least three-fourths of your worship attendees also participate in a Sunday school class or small group each week?

Diagnosis: Refer to page 17 to evaluate the severity of this emergency.

✚ PRESCRIPTION
Luke 4:16; 5:15; 6:12–13
1 Corinthians 3:1–6

✚ FIRST AID

The pastor must make an immediate declaration.

Pastors tend to be passionate about preaching and the Sunday morning worship service is the venue that affords the opportunity to exercise their gift before the largest number of people. The commitment and the call that they have motivates them to be the best that they can be, and they invest time in developing their skills. The pastor's love for preaching and the Sunday morning worship experience can have an unintended consequence.

The Sunday morning worship time accounts for the largest amount of participation of any ministry or gathering during the course of the week. The members come to worship and to hear the pastor deliver a sermon to help them in their spiritual growth and to live out their faith during the week. What an excellent way for a believer to begin the week! The preaching and the ministry of the pastor tend to connect him to the congregation in a unique way. The congregation grows to love the pastor as he instructs and ministers week by week. Sometimes an exceptionally skilled preacher will begin to draw a larger audience as members grow in their affection for his ministry and begin to enthusiastically invite friends and neighbors. The unintended consequence begins to unfold. The worship service begins to grow in attendance, enthusiasm, and importance. The Sunday school may grow slightly on the coattails of the increase in worship, but a gap begins to develop between the quality of the two ministries.

What happens when the pastor leaves? If the only point of connection has been the pastor, and if the quality of the Sunday school has endured months or years of neglect, you will likely experience a steep decline in attendance. It is time to think ahead. A pastor will leave eventually, even if he has no intention of doing so any time soon. The pastor needs to make an immediate declaration affirming the value of other relationships and connection points for the long-term health of the church. Sunday school or small groups is the logical way to help members make those additional connections. The pastor should preach a sermon, series of sermons, or at least make an immediate declaration affirming the importance and value of Sunday school as a key ministry for all members.

Begin to elevate Sunday school by all means.

The pastor's declaration is a starting point and should be done immediately and also frequently henceforth. Enhance his declaration by elevating the Sunday school through multiple sources. Here are a few ideas:

- Give a brief weekly Sunday school report prior to worship.

- Have a commissioning service for Sunday school teachers.

- Regularly write about Sunday school in newsletters, bulletins, and blogs.

- Preach a sermon or series focusing on the value of small groups.

- Develop a special day, month, or campaign to emphasize Sunday school.

- Initiate or improve training provided for current Sunday school leaders.

- Start and promote new Sunday school classes.

- Implement and promote a topic that will attract worship attendees to Sunday school.

- Utilize banners or signage to promote Sunday school opportunities.

- Regularly list classes available in church printed material.

- Conduct a phone blitz inviting every member for a special Sunday.

- Take a portion of the worship to divide everyone into groups for a brief meeting to make an initial connection with the leader and group that they belong to.

Incorporate several weeks of testimonies into the worship.

Incorporating testimonies is another way to immediately elevate the Sunday school. The strategy is given its own emphasis at this point because it may be the strongest way to elevate the Sunday school apart from the pastor's declaration and can be done immediately. Make time in your worship for several Sundays in a row for members to share testimonies of the way that the Sunday school ministry has ministered, blessed, encouraged, or helped them to grow in their faith and fellowship. Let the members hear from their peers about the value of the Sunday school from a perspective of personal application.

Be sure to utilize members representing all life stages for sharing these testimonies. Some worship attendees may not think that the ministry and opportunities are relevant to them unless it comes from someone in a similar life stage. You will do well to have each person sharing a testimony write it and share it with you in advance. More harm than good can be done if the testimony does not make the desired points or if it is delivered devoid of passion for Sunday school. A video testimony can serve the same purpose and allows for mistakes to be edited, length to be appropriately adjusted, and coaching to be given if the person sharing the testimony is inexperienced with public presentations. Ideally, the testimony will come from a member, but in rare circumstances it may have to come from a person of another healthy church if you lack Sunday school attendees from a particular age group.

Conduct an enrollment campaign in the worship service.

Be sure that all of those attending your worship on a regular basis are assigned to a Sunday school class. They are more likely to attend if they are receiving ministry as well as invitations not only to Bible study but to fellowship opportunities as well. An enrollment campaign is easy to do and can be conducted in the form of a survey on a typical Sunday morning. Be sure that index cards and pens or pencils are readily available in your worship service on the morning that you intend to conduct the following survey. The survey takes less than five minutes.

Ask each person to number one through six and ask them to record their answers as you guide them through the survey.

1. What is your first and last name?

2. Are you a member or a guest of our church?

3. Please write down a contact number in case the staff or church leader needs to ask a follow-up question.

4. What is your grade if you are in school or your age grouping if you are older than 18 (20s, 30s, 40s, 50s, or 60+)?

5. What is the name of your Sunday school teacher in our church? If you don't know the answer, leave this blank.

6. If you left number 5 blank, may we assign you to a group? Here is what will happen: The group will pray for you regularly, maintain contact in order to be aware of any needs you may have, invite you to their fellowships, and invite you to Bible study. We want you to attend Bible study, but even if you cannot, we want to be sure you are prayed for, ministered to, and invited to fellowships.

Following the survey, divide the cards according to the answer to number 5: the name of the Sunday school teacher. Compare the responses with existing Sunday school rolls. Feel free to enroll anyone who wrote the name of a teacher if they are not on that roll. They think they are for some reason, and you should feel free to oblige them. Many worship attendees will grant permission to be assigned to a class when answering number 6. Do you know what to do next? They must be assigned and immediately contacted and invited by leaders of the class to which they are assigned. Many will attend; all should be prayed for, ministered to, and invited to fellowships from this point forward. Does this guarantee that they will attend? No, but failing to pray, minister, and invite is almost a guarantee that they will not ever attend.

Utilize fellowships as a bridge.

People attend Sunday school because of Bible study and because of relationships. Some worship attendees, whether right or wrong, may assume they are getting enough Bible study from the pastor since he is doing such a great job in his preaching. However, relationships are not built in a worship setting. Relationships occur when there is interaction between people. A person can attend a worship service and have little or no conversation with other members. A person can easily be overlooked in larger settings because it is difficult to know who are members and who are guests. A small gathering allows for introductions, interaction, and discussion. People do not build relationships merely by being in the same room but by conversing and getting to know one another.

All people have a common desire for meaningful relationships. Sunday school leaders should be purposeful in helping existing, new, and prospective members in developing these friendships. Sunday school has a side door that can be a bridge for many to do so. The front door is the direct invitation for members and guests to attend the Sunday school. Perhaps you have done that and many have not responded. Many who will not respond to the direct invitation will respond to an opportunity to go out to eat, go to a party or recreational activity, or participate in some other social activity that is not directly related to a Bible study. Challenge your Sunday school leaders to plan and host frequent fellowship gatherings apart from the Sunday morning Bible study experience. The key is to invite guests as well as members to participate. Once a guest engages in fellowships, recognizes those who are part of the weekly Bible study gathering, and begins to connect with the members through fellowship, he or she can walk into the Sunday school through the side door of fellowship.

✚ REHAB
Teach the congregation that "it's not about the man."

A member with one point of connection will often be lost when that connection is broken. Suppose that a member attends worship each week because of affection for the pastor and his preaching ministry. (At this point no judgments are being made about the spirituality or maturity of that individual.) What happens when the pastor leaves? The church needs to be strategic in assisting all attendees to make multiple connection points. The Sunday school ministry can provide two additional points of connection.

A person who attends Sunday school begins to bond with the group that he or she meets with on a regular basis. The interaction that people experience on Sunday morning, the ministry they receive over the course of time, and the friendships that develop through fellowship connect them to the group. In addition, the Sunday school attendee begins to develop a connection to the Bible study teacher in the small group in a similar manner to that of a pastor. What happens to this person when the pastor leaves? The person still has a small group and a Bible teacher to whom he or she is connected. At least two connection points are still in place. What if it's the Sunday school teacher who resigns? At least two connection points still remain.

Members need to be taught that the first and foremost connection point is to Jesus Christ. The reality is that people should be committed because of Jesus and not because of the person standing in the pulpit. It is not about the man in the pulpit but about the One who gave His life that we might be redeemed. However, people live at all points along the line of maturity. Help them make multiple points of connection to assist them on that journey and to account for changes in leadership. Make the Sunday school a priority and strive to get everyone connected to a group.

Conduct honest evaluation and implement best practices.

Why are worship attendees not attending your Sunday school? Is it because it has been neglected, because it is weak, or because it is not a priority? Take time to honestly evaluate the Sunday school on its own merits and determine what needs to change. Do you have someone in your congregation or on your staff who has expertise in the dynamics of Sunday school health and growth? Ask that person to begin analysis and to make recommendations. If you do not have such a person, it may be necessary to bring in an outside consultant from your denomination, from a church with a healthy Sunday school, or a person with expertise in the field of Sunday school health and growth. An outside person may provide some objectivity that would serve the church well.

Sunday school is much more high maintenance than the worship service because there are so many moving parts. In addition, Sunday school classes are led by volunteers whereas worship is generally led by a pastor with extensive education and training. Leading the Sunday school to be healthy requires direct leadership, ongoing attention, and continual elevation by the pastor and key leaders. It is similar to your personal health in this way. In order to get in good physical shape you must exercise regularly, not just once or twice a year. You must be disciplined every week to get where you need to be. Though it takes months to get into shape, you need only neglect exercise for a few weeks to undo all that hard work. The slide backward goes so much faster than the march forward. The same is true with the Sunday school. Some practices cannot be neglected. Like most of my lists, this is not comprehensive, but you will not be able to lead the Sunday school forward without understanding and implementing the following practices:

1. Leaders must be trained on an ongoing basis.

2. The purpose must be rightly and regularly communicated. Sunday school is not just a Bible study but a strategy for the church to fulfill the Great Commission.

3. The pastor must support and elevate Sunday school as a priority.

4. The enrollment must expand and be viewed as a ministry list.

5. Everyone on the Sunday school rolls must receive regular contact, ministry, and invitations to fellowship.

6. Groups must be trained, challenged, and intentional in conducting outreach and follow-up of guests.

7. Adult classes must be intentional in developing and releasing leaders to serve in other areas.

8. New classes will have to be created to sustain growth.

9. Standards will have to be implemented to keep leaders ministering at a strong level.

10. New leaders must be enlisted and equipped throughout the year.

CHAPTER 9

We Have a Teacher Who Needs to Step Down

✚ THE EMERGENCY

What would you do? What would you do if you were the pastor or the director of the Sunday school and a teacher needed to step down? That may be putting it politely. Perhaps action needs to be taken to remove the Sunday school teacher because of a serious issue. How do you remove a volunteer? How do you remove a volunteer when you are a volunteer yourself? What would you do in the following circumstances?

1. Michael has been teaching an adult Sunday school class for about two years. He is well-liked and is gifted in his ability to communicate a lesson. He participates and cooperates in training activities and promotions when called upon by church leaders. You were surprised to discover that he has been teaching a doctrine that is in direct contradiction to the belief of your church and denomination. A conversation with him

confirms his stand; you had not heard incorrectly. He politely and yet boldly stands by what he is teaching. What would you do?

2. Lisa has been serving as a preschool teacher for many years. She has been a member of the church since she was a child. The children love her, and she does a great job inside the classroom. That is, once she shows up. She is never on time and usually arrives anywhere from five to fifteen minutes after Sunday school is scheduled to begin. In addition, she will miss several Sundays each year and does not bother to make arrangements or call anyone to communicate that she will not be present. What would you do?

3. Rico has been teaching the middle school boys class for a few months. He has never taught prior to this but seemed like a great candidate. He is a committed believer with a good attitude and a willing spirit. He is doctrinally sound and is usually one of the first teachers to arrive on Sunday morning. The problem occurs once the teaching begins. He literally reads the lesson from the teachers curriculum guide to the students. He is boring the students with an ineffective style, and you have noticed that the average attendance has been reduced by 50 percent since he began teaching. What would you do?

4. Paula and her husband have been teaching the college young adults for a couple of years. They do a great job of ministry, outreach, and teaching each week. You were surprised to learn recently that she and her husband were having some marital problems, though it sounds as if they were working through them. The shock was that the root of the problem may have been an inappropriate relationship with one of the college students. What would you do?

5. Tyler is a longtime member and teacher of Sunday school in the church. He is a leader, and many members look to him for guidance on church and spiritual issues. His teaching skills are fair and yet his class attendance stays strong due to the

ministry done by the class and the strong relationships. Tyler has a background in education and does not feel that teacher training is relevant for him. Many teachers appear to be taking his lead though several desperately need the training and all would benefit, including Tyler. What would you do?

✚ TRIAGE

1. Does your church have written policies describing procedures for addressing problems with volunteers, including Sunday school teachers?

2. Does your church have written guidelines or standards for Sunday school leaders?

3. Does your church have a written doctrinal statement that leaders can review prior to taking a leadership role?

4. Does your church conduct background screening and personal interviews with all volunteers?

5. Does your church require or expect Sunday school teachers to participate in training on a regular basis?

Diagnosis: Refer to page 17 to evaluate the severity of this emergency.

✚ PRESCRIPTION
Galatians 6:1–2; James 5:19–20
Matthew 5:23–26
2 Timothy 1:13–14; 2:1–7, 14–19, 23–26; 3:10–17; 4:1–5

✚ FIRST AID
Diagnose the severity of the issue.
The urgency of any action and the consequences of inappropriate behaviors are not the same in every circumstance.

The way in which you should address failure of a teacher to show up one Sunday and a severe moral failure on the part of another teacher will not be the same. Begin by diagnosing the severity of the issue. Consider the following questions to assist in your evaluation:

1. Is the issue related to the skills of the teacher? Proceed slowly if this is the case. The objective in this situation is to provide instruction, training, and resources to help the teacher develop the needed skills. Keep the leader in place as long as there is a willingness to improve and progress is being made in that direction. Assign a mentor or coach if necessary.

2. Is the issue related to the commitment level of the teacher? Proceed deliberately with deference to your church's written guidelines and standards. If your church does not have any written guidelines, then the teacher's actions are not the root of the problem. By leaving guidelines ambiguous, the teacher may not even realize that there is a problem. If guidelines *are* being violated, meet with the leader to discuss concerns, and give him or her the opportunity to explain the circumstances, to recommit, or—if the issue is negotiable—to come to an agreement.

3. Is the issue related to a doctrinal error? Proceed deliberately with deference to your church or denominational doctrinal statements. The Bible itself certainly takes precedence when considering doctrinal concerns. The challenge may be one of interpretation or opinion. A summary of doctrinal beliefs can serve to clarify the understanding and conviction of your church. You should respond immediately if the error contradicts a doctrinal essential, such as the deity of Christ or the exclusivity of Christ for salvation. You should respond cautiously if the error is not

essential to Christian faith, such as timing of events like the rapture or the meaning of symbolism found in the apocalyptic Scriptures. You may need to agree to disagree while coming to an understanding that the leader will not deliberately or overtly contradict the local church's conviction on the issue. You should respond with grace if the issue is related to preference. Believers sometimes take their own experiences or traditions and elevate them to a level of conviction that is not supported by Scripture. Be cautious not to alienate a great leader over issues such as music style or furniture preferences.

4. Is the issue related to a severe violation of Scripture or moral failure? Take action immediately when a leader is involved in a moral failure or commits a severe violation of Scripture. The aim should always be to bring believers to repentance and restoration. However, leaving someone in a role of leadership when he or she has deliberately chosen to engage in actions in direct violation of Scripture can have an adverse affect on the ability of your congregation to minister in your community. Pray for discernment with the understanding that while the error cannot be overlooked an appropriate degree of privacy and confidentiality should be maintained when and if possible.

Work with key leaders through the process.

If the issue is serious enough to warrant the teacher's removal either immediately or at some point in the future, you'll need to get key leaders involved. You will do well to address minor issues personally and major issues with the counsel and wisdom of other church leaders. Taking unilateral action to remove a volunteer is not ordinarily acceptable in most volunteer organizations such as a church. There is certainly less leverage for handling difficulties with volunteers than with those who are compensated for their service. A person who receives compensation likely has a designated supervisor or team with the authority to take swift action when problems arise. So how do you keep teachers accountable?

Bringing key leaders into the process has several benefits. First, circumstances can be evaluated with more accuracy. Perhaps other leaders have information that you do not. Second, objectivity is maximized by including other leaders. Addressing problems unilaterally may be interpreted as a personal attack or personality conflict. Third, involving others adds gravity to the process. The fact that a group of leaders has a concern rather than just an individual helps the offender understand the seriousness of the issue. Fourth, bringing in other leaders provides protection for the leader of the Sunday school ministry. Perhaps you are a volunteer Sunday school director yourself. Moving from simple inquiry to potential action may require the endorsement of other key leaders to accomplish.

Consider implications without compromising convictions.

Suppose a pastor or Sunday school director has been serving in that role for only a few months. What if the teacher who needs to be dealt with has been serving for fifteen years? That pastor or director would do well to proceed with much caution. The swiftness of action will be dramatically different if the pastor or director has been in the role for fifteen years and the teacher for only a few months. What are the implications for your leadership if you are new in your position and need to confront a long-tenured teacher? Do not hesitate to immediately tackle issues related to moral failure, severe violations of Scripture, or teaching that contradicts essential doctrines. However, other issues may need to be overlooked or addressed more casually, so long as biblical convictions are not violated. You may, for example, not appreciate that a teacher is often late, but you may or may not want to make an issue of it at this point.

Pray for wisdom in knowing which problems to confront and when to confront them.

Another possible implication is the loss of members. You always risk losing the volunteer as a leader, even if the issue is minor. The person may take offense at the confrontation no matter how mild. But in addition, you may also lose the person who is confronted as a member of your church. Is it possible that the teacher will influence others in the congregation and that division will arise and families may be lost? I'm not suggesting that you do not need to address the leader—and the more severe the issue the more important it is that corrective measures are taken—but consider the implications prior to taking action. The congregation may be better served if the person is removed or chooses to leave. Place the protection of your church's biblical convictions and reputation first, but do not neglect to weigh implications when addressing issues which although important are negotiable in the short term.

Take caution against neglecting scriptural precepts.

What does the Bible have to say about the issue at hand? What does Scripture teach about the restoration of believers who have failed? The teaching of the Scripture absolutely takes precedence in all of the circumstances described in this chapter. The suggestions that I am sharing are based on experience, wisdom, and practical application for dealing with volunteers. Ignoring problems or failing to confront difficult situations will not make them go away. Balancing compassion and confrontation is a challenge for all leaders. Study the Scripture, pray for wisdom, and seek to address problems with Christ-honoring integrity.

✚ REHAB
Talk through the process before there is a problem.

What would you do? You previously read a number of scenarios asking how you would address a variety of problems that can occur with Sunday school teachers. Confronting the problems can be awkward, stressful, and, if not handled correctly, detrimental to relationships and the reputation of a church. Sometimes it is better to talk about a problem when there is not a problem. Consider taking the scenarios provided and discuss them at a meeting of your Sunday school leaders. You can conduct the discussion somewhat more objectively since you did not create the scenarios.

Get insight from your current leaders on methods and procedures for addressing problems that may arise. Consider using what is learned in the discussion to develop agreed-upon guidelines for future reference. Engage your teachers in this discussion, or, in larger settings select a team from among your leaders who in turn present the guidelines, methods, and procedures to your teachers. A process such as this will not eliminate conflict but may reduce some of the stress involved since the manner for addressing problems was developed and agreed upon by Sunday school teachers from your church.

Establish written standards and guidelines.

Many problems that churches have with Sunday school teachers are simple failure of communication. Written standards can assist you in dealing with problems much more objectively. Although you may be exercising objectivity, it is easy for someone to take your "opinions" as a personal attack. Applying church guidelines will lessen, though not eliminate, the personal nature of any confrontation. Do you have teachers who arrive late each week? Find the document that describes what time their arrival is expected and underline that section. Do you have teachers who do not participate in training? Underline the section of the document that describes the church's expectations regarding the number of hours or frequency of involvement in training. If you cannot place your hands on these documents you are postured for greater difficulty in addressing leadership concerns.

As you develop guidelines for your leaders you should be cautious about a few things. First, take care to list the minimum standards. Your guidelines should not have twenty or thirty points. You will overwhelm your leaders if you have too many rules. Second, be cautious about asking your leaders to sign the documents at first implementation. Begin by introducing guidelines, enlisting future leaders with these guidelines as standards, and perhaps inviting leaders to sign as they grow accustomed to the standards (and with much advance notice). Third, don't fear raising expectations. Churches that have no expectations or low expectations of Sunday school teachers will experience little or no commitment on behalf of the volunteers and much more difficulty addressing problem teachers.

Engage all of your teachers or call together a group of teachers to serve on a team. Assign at least one teacher from all of the age groupings: preschoolers, children, youth, and adults. Ask them to develop minimum standards to serve as guidelines and expectations of teachers as well as procedures for dealing with difficult situations. Consider including the following:

1. What time are teachers expected to arrive each week?

2. What records and reports are needed from leaders each week?

3. What are expectations regarding use of curriculum and preparation each week?

4. What frequency of participation in training is expected?

5. What is expected of teachers regarding class organization, leadership, and outreach?

6. What are the procedures if a teacher must be absent?

7. What are the expectations related to church involvement apart from Sunday school?

8. Is a doctrinal statement or summary available that teachers are expected to affirm?

CHAPTER 10

Our Teachers Are Boring

✚ THE EMERGENCY

Bumper stickers posted on vehicles can serve to inform, amuse, provoke, or opine on an endless number of issues. Perhaps you have seen a bumper sticker promoting a church with some slogan such as "Follow me to First Community Church." You certainly would never want to see a bumper sticker with your church name on it describing your Sunday school such as the ones that follow:

First Community Sunday School:
Once You Have Been, You Will Never Go Again!

First Community Sunday School:
Introducing a Logical Solution to Your Insomnia!

First Community Church:
I "Once" Went to Their Sunday School!

First Community Sunday School: The First Teachers to
Make Ben Stein (Bueller, Bueller) Sound Passionate!

I SURVIVED FIRST COMMUNITY SUNDAY SCHOOL!

FIRST COMMUNITY SUNDAY SCHOOL:
MORE FUN THAN A ROOT CANAL!

FIRST COMMUNITY SUNDAY SCHOOL:
BEEN THERE, DONE THAT!

FIRST COMMUNITY SUNDAY SCHOOL:
BOTH MEMBERS WERE REALLY NICE!

FOLLOW ME TO FIRST COMMUNITY SUNDAY SCHOOL—
ON THE WAY TO A GOOD RESTAURANT!

I ATTEND FIRST COMMUNITY SUNDAY SCHOOL
AND FUNERAL HOME

I ATTENDED FIRST COMMUNITY SUNDAY SCHOOL
AND WOKE UP A TEACHER!

FIRST COMMUNITY SUNDAY SCHOOL: THEY AIN'T GOT NO CLASS

✚ TRIAGE

1. Do you provide training for your teachers on a regular basis?

2. Are your Sunday school teachers expected to participate in training?

3. Do you regularly have first-time guests visit the Sunday school?

4. Do first-time guests to your Sunday school typically return?

5. Are the majority of your Sunday school teachers skilled and passionate in their teaching?

Diagnosis: Refer to page 17 to evaluate the severity of this emergency.

✚ PRESCRIPTION

1 Corinthians 9:19–23	Psalm 78:1–8
2 Timothy 1:6	Ephesians 4:11–16
Deuteronomy 11:18–21	2 Timothy 4:1–4

✚ FIRST AID

Identify the roots of the problem.

Some people have the impression that Sunday school is boring. Other people believe that Bible study is boring. The reality is that there is no such thing as a boring Sunday school, boring curriculum, or boring Bible study. However, there are boring presentations given by teachers. Why are your Sunday school teachers boring? The real question is, why are they making boring presentations?

Begin by identifying the root of the problem. A presentation is generally the result of a combination of three issues: spiritual passion, skills, and preparation. Failure in any of these three areas will almost always result in a boring presentation. Your church may have a "corporate culture" that is weak in one or more of these areas, and then you will have an overall climate of boring Sunday school led by boring teachers.

A lack of personal spiritual growth on the part of teachers will result in passionless or boring teaching. The best teaching comes from overflow, and overflow is the result of growing in knowledge and intimacy with Christ. How sad it is that many people perceive church or Sunday school to be boring because Sunday school teachers lack passion for sharing the best news in the world. Are your teachers growing in their faith? They cannot lead the members where they are not going themselves.

Many Sunday school teachers do have a growing and abiding love for the Lord but lack the skills to teach effectively. Weakness in skills can be directly related to neglect in training, either on the part of the teacher to participate or on the part of the church leaders to provide it. Why do church leaders assume that volunteers know how to teach skillfully? The skills do not come by osmosis or all teachers would possess them. Do your teachers participate in training in order to develop and refine their skills in communicating God's Word?

Possessing passion and skills will not be enough if a leader fails in weekly preparation. A teacher need not spend dozens of hours each week getting ready to lead a class. However, throwing together a quick plan on Saturday night cannot be compensated for with passion that is not applied or skills that cannot be maximized.

Neglect in preparation can be related to skills or may be symptomatic of another church issue. Sunday school teachers represent some of the best leaders in the church, and they may often be connected to multiple leadership roles. Once you add the additional responsibilities to family, work, and the routines of life, it is no wonder that preparation for Sunday suffers. Is it possible that the church is stretching the teachers too thin by asking too much of their time in other areas? Have teachers been taught preparation and time-management skills through the Sunday school leader training plan? . . .*What's that? Your church has no training plan for your teachers?* That is the root of the problem!

Provide immediate tools and instruction.

You can provide immediate help by providing the tools and instruction that your teachers need. The immediate resources will not resolve the problems but will aid leaders in improving their skills. Every step of improvement will make a difference, and you have to start somewhere. Here are possible ways that you can provide immediate help:

1. Invite a guest (expert) to come and provide instruction. You need three to four weeks to promote such an opportunity but need not wait for months to do so. The guest might be someone from a church in proximity to your community, a denominational leader with expertise in Sunday school, or a consultant who specializes in Sunday school or Bible teaching. When do you gather with the leaders? Sunday afternoon? Saturday morning? Monday night? You gather when the maximum number of your teachers can be present.

2. Offer your teachers a series to help them to hone their teaching skills. You can purchase a variety of resources to give your teachers a jump start on improvement. *Teaching with Style* by Bruce Wilkinson is a great introductory series designed to help Bible teachers communicate God's Word effectively.

3. Take your leaders to a conference specializing in Sunday school. A well-led conference has the effect of fast forwarding their training experience. Encourage your church to make an investment in your teachers and your Sunday school by covering the expenses for your teachers if possible.

4. Place a book in the hands of your teachers that will help them grow in their skills. The advantages are that the resource can be in their hands quickly, can be read on their own schedule, and can provide common ground for follow-up discussion. Consider gathering in a home or over a meal to discuss the book as well as to reward those who read and participate.

5. Provide video or audio training resources to your teachers that they can view on their own schedule. Depending on the cost of the resources, these may need to be shared and passed around. Follow up as discussed in number 4.

Offer evaluation for individuals or the group.

If done correctly, evaluation can prompt improvement. You can conduct evaluation in a number of ways. One possibility is evaluation of *group* strengths and weaknesses. Announce a visit to each Sunday school class by a director, staff member, or designee assigned to conduct the evaluation. Assure teachers that the purpose of the evaluation is to identify group patterns, rather than individual evaluation; this can relieve pressure and anxiety. Follow up by providing analysis of patterns discovered, along with suggestions for overall improvement that all teachers should be encouraged to apply.

A second approach is to provide *personal* evaluation and recommendations for improvement. Invite teachers to permit a leader to either attend or view a video of the class. A skilled, diplomatic evaluation can assist each teacher in making immediate and substantial improvements.

A third approach is to survey members of the Sunday school, seeking their analysis of teacher strengths and weaknesses. Again, a general analysis of the group will be less threatening. Use caution if using this method to evaluate teachers individually. The results can be much more painful when coming from members who attend weekly compared with a more objective analysis by someone outside the class.

✚ REHAB

Stop neglecting and assuming.

A sad fact is that many churches enlist Sunday school leaders, assign them to a class, provide them with curriculum, and send them to lead their designated group. The experiences and the education of those assigned to teach vary from person to person. The degree of success is affected by many factors, including passion, preparation skills, communication skills, time invested in the class, and relationship skills. Most importantly, the leader and the class must be filled with the Holy Spirit and committed to spiritual growth. A group may overlook the poor teaching of a leader with strong relational skills where much time is invested in ministry. Many Sunday schools struggle because church leaders assume that the teachers know what to do and how to do it.

How are your Sunday school teachers prepared to conduct their ministry? What is the training plan in your church? Are teachers expected to participate in training? Buckle up for this next statement: The reason that the teachers in your church are boring is the fault of the leaders if training is not being provided. The leaders have wrongly assumed that enlistment and assignment of Sunday school teachers is sufficient. The neglect of training has allowed a culture of low expectations and ineffective methods. Don't take offense, but rather be challenged. Read Ephesians 4:11–16 and take note of the responsibility of leaders to equip the members to conduct their ministries. Teachers are not supposed to be boring, and Sunday school does not have to be lifeless. Make a commitment to stop assuming that leaders know what to do and stop neglecting leader training.

Focus on "what" as well as "why" and "how" in training.

Training comes to the surface over and over when addressing problems in Sunday school. Equipping leaders can circumvent many problems, address problems when they do arise, improve the skills of the leaders, and provide healthy accountability. Equipping is a biblical responsibility that gives the Sunday school ministry practical results. Effective training should include times of inspiration, instruction, and information. The subjects that need to be addressed are numerous and must be repeated within a couple of years because new teachers have been enlisted, some will fall back into old habits, and perhaps others were not present when a particular topic was previously addressed.

My previous book, *Sunday School That Really Works*, addresses the following subjects in detail and could serve as one possible source for instructional material. This list is not intended to be exhaustive but to serve as a template for planning the topics of your training aimed specifically at improving teaching skills in the coming year.

1. Understanding the purpose of Sunday school

2. Your spiritual growth: the foundation of effective teaching

3. How to make best use of curriculum and resources in preparation

4. Creating a great environment

5. Preparing an age-appropriate Bible study

6. Teacher time management: making the most of preparation time

7. Teaching methods

8. How to maximize interaction and participation

9. How to ensure application of the Bible study

10. Common teaching mistakes and how to avoid them

Keep in mind that a healthy Sunday school is centered on good teaching but is the result of effectiveness in organization, outreach, ministry, and fellowship as well. Equipping is never complete because many dynamics are at work in a healthy Sunday school and rarely are they ever conquered in totality.

Initiate safeguards.

Do not ever go back. Do not allow your Sunday school to be perceived as boring. Initiate safeguards to keep from drifting back to an ineffective, lifeless, or boring climate.

The first safeguard is to prioritize the Sunday school ministry as a key strategy for your church in fulfilling the Great Commission. If it falls way down on the list of priorities in your church, it will be easy to accept or fall back into unhealthy habits.

The second safeguard is continual analysis and honest evaluation. The Sunday school director or key leader of your Sunday school ministry should be given this mandate from this point forward.

Third, the equipping must be systematic and progress in quality in the same manner that you desire for the skills of your teachers to grow. Develop training in twelve-month blocks and meet with teachers for training several times each year. Invite everyone, promote diligently, and apply with dedication whether attended by many or few.

CHAPTER 11

We Are Completely Out of Space

✚ THE EMERGENCY

Lack of space to conduct a Sunday school ministry is a nuisance at best and a barrier to growth at worst. Both the quantity and the quality of the space can be a hindrance. Quality is measured by how clean the space is, how cluttered the space is, and how contemporary the space is. Don't be thrown off by the word *contemporary* in this instance. Although a retro feel to the space can stir pleasant sentiments for some, it may not be the best way to reach new people for your Sunday school ministry.

The specific issue being addressed in this emergency, however, relates to the quantity of the space available. A room that measures about 200 square feet should comfortably accommodate a class of ten adults. Consider where you stand with this amount of space based on current average attendance.

- Zero attendance: You need to start a class in this room.

- One to Three: This small group needs to get very aggressive with outreach.

- Four to Five: Space is no problem. The group will grow close but needs to reach out to others.

- Six to Seven: Space is still not a problem. A group of this size can begin to organize and generate some momentum in outreach and ministry.

- Eight to Ten: Great size for a group in a small or medium-size church. Large churches tend to have slightly larger classes. Once the class averages ten, it is at 80 percent capacity. A couple of chairs are still available.

- Eleven to Twelve: The room is full and the class is excited. Maybe they can squeeze a couple more chairs into the room.

- Thirteen to Fourteen: What an awesome class! The room is packed and the enthusiasm is contagious. However, no guests are ever present. The members have no motivation to invite because there is no room for guests to attend.

- Fifteen to Sixteen: Guests were present for the high attendance day. The class sat hip to hip, and those with claustrophobia barely made it. Now you know how sardines feel.

- Seventeen to Eighteen: Officials from the *Guinness Book of World Records* were present to snap a photo to go alongside the classic picture of college students packed into a Volkswagen. You will not want this picture to be published.

- Nineteen to Twenty: Couldn't happen. Josh Hunt once posed the question: How many pickles can you put in a ten-pickle jar? You may squeeze in eleven or twelve, but you cannot put twenty pickles in there. Growth ceased long before you reached nineteen in a room of this size.

✚ TRIAGE

1. Do you have a least one vacant room currently available to begin a new class?

2. Do your members have an attitude of flexibility about changing rooms or schedules?

3. Do you regularly evaluate space to ensure that the classes are assigned to rooms suited to the average attendance of the group?

4. Do all of your classrooms have additional room to grow or for guests to attend?

5. Are you attentive to the quality of the space as well as the quantity?

Diagnosis: Refer to page 17 to evaluate the severity of this emergency.

✚ PRESCRIPTION

James 2:1–9   Luke 18:15-17
Isaiah 53:2–3

✚ FIRST AID

Conduct a preliminary analysis of the space.

A detailed analysis will need to be conducted as you consider long-term steps; however, you may be out of space right now and need to respond to an emergency situation. Here are three ways to conduct a preliminary analysis within a week to provide you with information needed to initiate adjustments:

1. Are there any vacant rooms available to start new classes? If the answer is "no" then you are out of space. You may be able to rearrange some space or find other meeting space possibilities but you know that you have an issue now or will have one shortly if there are no vacant rooms available. The absence of a vacant room makes it more challenging to create a new class and to reassign rooms such as moving a growing class to a larger area. Either of these can be a hindrance to growth.

2. Conduct a Sunday morning walk-through of your facilities. Yogi Berra once said, "You can observe a lot by watching." Take the staff or a couple of key leaders on a Sunday morning tour from the exterior to the interior. Look at everything with the eyes of a guest. For example: How are the signs? If your facility is small and your members know where everything is, you may think that's irrelevant. Signs are not for the members, however; they are for the guests. Take a quick look into each class to see which are crowded and which have room to spare. Are some small classes in larger rooms and some of the larger classes in smaller rooms? Take notes and discuss what immediate adjustments can be made.

3. Conduct a paper analysis of your Sunday school space. Take or make a drawing of your facilities and consider every place where a group could meet. Write the enrollment and the average attendance of each group on the drawing. Evaluate group sizes in relation to the assigned space, proximity of various age groups to the worship area, and potential spaces for expansion or new classes. What adjustments are possible?

Communicate the current status and the barriers to the congregation.

Many of your members may not see the problem. They may be comfortable where they are and quite content with the space in which they meet. Prepare your congregation for immediate and future adjustments with the following:

1. Communicate the priority of the Great Commission. One of the options for dealing with space difficulties is to do nothing. However, that is not an option in the context of your obligation to Christ's command to reach out to all nations beginning in your own community. You must reach and disciple. Sunday school is not only a tool but also a strategy to assist the congregation in their obedience. Space must be provided in order for the Sunday school to grow.

2. Communicate your findings from the preliminary analysis. Ask the congregation for their input and observations and for a commitment to flexibility in making necessary adjustments. Communicate that although every current group will not be immediatcly affected, all should assume that they will not be in their current location within the next few years. Remind them that the reason for their move will be a reflection of good news. People will have been reached and many will have trusted Christ as Savior prompting adjustments in space to accommodate the growth.

3. Communicate the consequences of inaction. Share that a failure to reach new people will ultimately result in decline. As time goes by the congregation will have members that move to other communities, go on to be with the Lord, and perhaps some who waver in their commitment or join other churches. Failure to conduct evangelism and outreach will result in decline and ultimately the demise of a local church.

Though the congregation is close and familiar with one another they must understand that it is awkward for guests to feel crowded. Caution the congregation against letting their personal sentimentality for a classroom, furniture, schedules, or buildings stand in the way of God's kingdom purposes. Ask the members to remove any barrier to fulfillment of the Great Commission.

Identify two more places for additional classes to meet.

Two more spaces will provide the flexibility that is needed. You can create new classes to relieve space in larger and growing groups as well as provide flexibility for shifting classes to rooms that provide for their growth.

First, consider adding a class to unused space such as the choir room or fellowship hall. You might even consider adding portable walls to the fellowship area if resources are immediately available. If not, add the idea to long-term solutions.

Second, consider areas such as offices or storage areas. You may need to purchase a portable storage building to shift some supplies or allow a part-time staff member to share space or work from home. It is not recommended that a full-time staff member's office space be used as an alternative.

Third, consider using the worship area for a Sunday school class. The space is not ideal if there are pews because of inflexibility in set-up. In addition, the class will be interrupted by early arrivers for worship. Meeting in the worship area is a temporary solution that can be done without expense and can be implemented immediately. Some of the alternatives that you will learn under long-term solutions might also be applied at this point.

✚ REHAB

Conduct a detailed analysis of the space.

A detailed space analysis should take all types of space

into consideration. The challenge is to provide balance. A congregation is generally limited to the smallest of these five areas: parking, property, worship space, education space, and fellowship space. An undersized fellowship space is the least problematic but can become a greater hindrance as growth continues. The numbers provided below are guidelines. You can violate the margins and continue to grow, but the further you stray from the numbers the more difficult the growth climb will become.

1. Parking: Count the paved and marked spaces and multiply times two. That is the parking capacity for your facility. The smaller the congregation the less relevant that number will be. You may have an attendance of thirty with no paved parking; however, you are not likely to accommodate several hundred without paved parking.

2. Property: Determine the acreage of the church excluding cemeteries or other areas where building is not permissible. To find the average capacity of your property, multiply the acreage times 100 for single-level buildings and times 125 for multilevel buildings.

3. Fellowship Space: Measure your fellowship area, excluding the kitchen, to determine the square footage. Divide the total square footage by 15 if you have round tables and by 12 if the tables are rectangular; that is the total capacity of your fellowship space.

4. Worship Space: For pews, measure the length of the pews in inches, excluding the choir loft. Divide the total inches of pews by 21 and then multiply times .80. Do the same for the choir area but do not multiply times .80. Add the two together—choir capacity plus congregation capacity—to

determine the comfortable seating capacity of your worship area. You could accommodate more but will sacrifice some comfort. For chairs, count the total number and multiply times .80 for the congregation, then add the total number in the choir loft. Multiplying times .80 (determining 80 percent of capacity) is significant because guests are not as likely to be invited when a room is completely full. This will allow for surges in attendance.

5. Education Space: You will need to measure and determine square footage for each individual room, whether occupied or vacant. The numbers vary by age group. Although they are smaller, younger age groups require more room per person than adults: children and preschoolers need more furniture than adults, and preschoolers also require more room to move around. Divide square footage of preschool rooms by 35, children's rooms by 25, and youth or adult rooms by 15. Take the total and multiply times .80 to determine average capacity. These numbers are based on optimum conditions and may be reduced by about five each if necessary. Again, multiplying times 80 percent keeps each room positioned to allow for growth and surges in attendance.

You should end up with a total for all five of these critical areas: parking, property, worship space, education space, and fellowship space. Which turned out to have the smallest capacity? Are the numbers similar, or are they way out of balance? They do not need to be exactly the same, and your worship area will likely be the largest; however, if the worship seating capacity is twice the amount of parking or education space available, you are not likely to ever fill the space on a regular basis. Is it impossible? No. But it is improbable, and the climb for growth will be difficult.

Consider and prioritize alternatives for adding classes.

What do you do when you are out of Sunday school space? You should acquaint yourself with all of the alternatives and prioritize your preferences. None are ideal and all have their own strengths and weaknesses. What can you do in addition to the alternatives discussed under the preceding section on immediate steps?

1. Use a master teacher format. Assign three or more groups of a similar life stage to a large area such as a fellowship hall. Assign a gifted teacher to share a message for about twenty minutes. The groups divide up for discussion and fellowship following the presentation.

2. Purchase or lease one or more mobile classrooms. The interior quality can be equivalent to a permanent structure but the exterior appearance is sometimes inferior. This can be done more quickly and inexpensively than construction, but the value of the unit depreciates quickly.

3. Begin one or more groups off campus. Perhaps the college group could meet at an alternative time and location. Could a young adult group meet in a home or business adjoining your property? The students might be able to meet at a local school. Off-campus groups can meet at alternative times or simultaneously. The off-campus solution can be more inconvenient but can often be done quickly, inexpensively, and temporarily. Should you go to a total home group approach? A congregation with no facilities should certainly do so. In an established setting, however, be cautious about dismantling the Sunday school to move to a total home group approach. It is not easier, and it comes with drawbacks. Among those drawbacks are the difficulty of accommodating the needs of young children off campus;

a lower percentage of worship attendees participating; and finding homes to accommodate all the groups. However, your church would do well to *add* home groups as an extension of the Sunday school ministry to reach more of your community, whether to alleviate space concerns or not. The climate that is created in small groups is critical. Whether groups meet on or off campus, committed leaders, consistent equipping, and an appropriate level of accountability are required.

4. Conducting multiple Sunday schools is another option. Yes, it can be done. It is the ideal solution for those congregations that have two worship services. Half of the members would go to Sunday school and then worship while the other half would go to worship first and then Sunday school. Several months of preparation are necessary, and the counsel of leaders from another church currently using the schedule that you anticipate will assist you greatly in avoiding the same mistakes that they may have made.

5. Construction of additional facilities is the solution that most congregations seek. The new facilities can meet the need of and add new life to the Sunday school ministry if the Sunday school is healthy. People will not attend simply because new facilities are built. Buildings are only tools and will not be of value unless the people who meet in them share the gospel and minister to the community. The disadvantages are the time and resources needed. Construction is a long-term solution and is rarely accomplished without implementing other alternatives during an interim period.

Initiate an annual "Realignment Sunday."

Realignment Sunday should be scheduled on opening day of the new Sunday school year, which typically coincides with the new school year. Promote preschoolers, children, and students to their new classes on realignment day. Endeavor to start at least one new class to reach people untouched by the existing groups. Adjust or change the signs on all adult classes so that they reflect the actual age group or life stage meeting in that particular space. Finally, consider the current layout and reassign rooms to ensure that the right classes are in the rooms most appropriate to their size.

The first through third grade class may be much smaller than the fourth and fifth grade class. Even if the first through third grades have been in the same room for the past few years it may be more appropriate to switch with the fourth and fifth grade class for the coming year.

Asking adult classes to move can be quite a challenge—likely the result of failure to communicate purpose and a lack of movement over the course of many years. Moving a group after a decade of assumed ownership of a room is like major surgery. An annual "realignment Sunday" can minimize the conflict because movement is anticipated. Conduct your space analysis annually leading up to Realignment Sunday and make adjustments a normal part of your church culture. Your future growth depends on it!

CHAPTER 12

We Have a Class That Will Not Cooperate

✚ THE EMERGENCY

An uncooperative class can be anything from a mild inconvenience to a potential cancer on the attitude of all classes in the future. Having every class on board is obviously preferable to having a rebel group going its own way. Lack of cooperation can take many forms but here are some serious and a couple of not-so-serious examples:

1. A class needs to be moved but puts up resistance because it has invested in upgrades and decorations for their room over the years.

2. A teacher refuses or intentionally neglects to organize the class and to engage in outreach.

3. A senior adult class refuses to halt the practice of rolling the pastor's lawn with toilet paper on every month that includes a fifth Saturday.

4. A growing class refuses to release members to serve in other areas or to help create a new class.

5. A teacher ignores or refuses to abide by established standards.

6. A group often holds impromptu church business meetings in the class to discuss church problems and recently replaced a picture of the Last Supper with a dart board that has a picture of the present Sunday school director on it.

7. A class refuses to participate in a Sunday school emphasis or campaign.

8. A class does not keep or report information or records needed by church leaders.

9. A teacher or a class consistently arrives late or holds the class late, disrupting the transition to the worship hour.

10. A teacher refuses to participate in any type of training provided by the staff or church.

✚ TRIAGE

1. Do you have a list of written standards or guidelines for your Sunday school leaders?

2. Are your Sunday school teachers expected to participate in training?

3. Do the pastor and the Sunday school director intentionally invest in relationship-building with Sunday school leaders?

4. Does your church have an agreed upon plan for dealing with problem Sunday school teachers?

5. Do all of your Sunday school teachers understand the purpose of Sunday school?

Diagnosis: Refer to page 17 to evaluate the severity of this emergency.

✚ PRESCRIPTION
James 1:5
1 Corinthians 1:10
Ephesians 4:11–16

✚ FIRST AID
Evaluate severity and implications before taking action.

Have you ever been inspired with a great idea? You read an idea, hear about something in training, or have that "light bulb turned on over your head" moment as you are driving down the road. The idea makes perfect sense to you, and you have no doubt that others will be inspired also. The idea is presented to your leaders and everyone is excited and on board. Everyone, that is, except for the group at the end of the hallway on the right. You have a James Dean class. The teacher of the class takes pride in being a rebel without a cause. The class likes to go its own way, and it does not matter if everyone else is cooperative. They act as if they are above the idea, too spiritual, or simply independent.

First, you need to determine if the challenge you are facing is a teacher problem or a class problem. A teacher is always involved, but often the group simply reflects the attitude of the leader. If you determine that the teacher is the primary problem, refer to chapter 9, "We Have a Teacher Who Needs to Step Down." Sometimes the teacher is responding to the wishes or the sentiments of the class as a whole.

The next step is to determine if the resistance is that of a single class or group of classes. The larger the number of classes that do not desire to cooperate, the more likely that the issue or idea either does not have merit, that the timing is not right, or that the groups were not prepared enough in advance for the change or the challenge. If several classes are uncooperative, you may need to step back and reconsider timing, preparation, or the entire idea.

Suppose that you have certainty that the idea or issue is critical and yet several classes are resisting. The problem in this case is not the idea but the preparation and timing. Some groups need time to get used to an idea. Others have questions but will be ready to get on board once their questions are answered. Preparation and timing are always important when introducing something new. I recently had a pastor call in a panic because several teachers balked at his idea of signing a teacher commitment form. I discovered that no standards or guidelines were ever in place in the church and the teachers were expected to sign upon introduction of the idea. The idea had merit, but the preparation and the timing were not well planned. Many months—sometimes years—are required to get leaders to that point of expectation.

Choose your battles carefully.

Once the severity and the implications have been considered, you will need to determine how to proceed. You will not want to scrap the idea entirely if you have only one or two uncooperative classes. You may believe that the issue is critical to the health of your church and determine that you need to press forward in spite of resistance on the part of several classes. Do you need to press on, back up, or back off of the idea? Be cautious about backing off of an idea once it has been introduced. Your credibility might be at stake if you do not follow through on a decision that you made as a leader. Backing up may be the solution. Making compromises on timing and depth of implementation can be a win–win if handled skillfully. James 1:5 says, "If any of you lacks wisdom, let him ask of God, who gives to all liberally and without reproach, and it will be given to him."

Do you need to press on? You will need God's wisdom and strength to do so. You have to determine how to deal with the uncooperative group. Does the group or the teacher have influence over others? Will a decision on their part not to cooperate make a significant difference? I once consulted with a Sunday school director who had an uncooperative class. The class consisted of three or four senior adults occupying a room that was very large and would have made a great space for a growing class. The senior adult class consisted of the church's oldest members and the class had a much larger attendance in years past. I advised the Sunday school director to leave them alone. I pointed out respectfully that the problem would resolve itself in the next year or so. The class will be down to one or two very soon and they will likely combine with the other senior adult class. The room will be vacated and no one will be upset. Do not get me wrong: You do not need to avoid confrontation just because someone will get upset, but you do need to choose your battles carefully.

Temper your expectations for the short term.

You are considering immediate steps or first aid at this point. The ultimate solution may require more time. You can accomplish your objectives but perhaps not immediately. What is the objective in this case? What do you want to accomplish? Would it be possible to divide the objective into several steps?

Suppose that you have a growing class running out of space. You have a great idea! You determine that the class would be an excellent source of leadership to create and launch a new class to reach more people. You introduce the great idea to the class with a smile on your face . . . and depart with a frown after being accused of nothing short of demon possession. The teacher and the class circle the wagons and do not want to cooperate.

In this case, the objective is to create a new class with the help of a growing class. Consider the following incremental steps to get to the ultimate objective:

1. Enlist a prospective teacher to start a new class.

2. Ask the teacher of the growing class to mentor and groom the prospective teacher for future ministry. Explain to the existing teacher that you chose him or her because you wanted the best possible leader to provide guidance.

3. Ask the group to pray about releasing two or three couples to start a new class in the coming months.

4. Ask the teacher to announce his or her endorsement for releasing two or three couples to start a new class. Ask him or her to share that no offense will be taken but that the change will be accepted as a compliment to his or her leadership.

5. Ask the class members to pray about whether they would be one of the couples to spend twelve months helping launch the new class.

6. Work with the teacher to directly enlist one or more couples for the new class.

7. Launch the new class.

Your objective has changed at this point. A victory is accomplished if you can enlist a prospective teacher to create a new class. Temper your expectations for the short term if possible and move toward the objective incrementally.

✚ REHAB
Invest in personal relationships with leaders.

Do your Sunday school teachers trust you? They will trust your ideas and your decisions if they trust you. Where does that trust come from? You will be trusted by those who know you, know your heart, know your motives, and know your vision. You can announce it if you wish, but that will not engender trust. An investment in personal relationships can make an immense difference over the course of time.

Perhaps you are new as the Sunday school director or the pastor and have essentially inherited a group of Sunday school leaders. You may be facing circumstances where poor leadership habits have developed over the years and many may be entrenched in the thinking of former leaders. Although you have a grasp of best practices for a healthy Sunday school, you may find yourself facing resistance. Choose your battles carefully in the early stages and get started on developing personal relationships with your leaders.

You will find it significantly easier to lead those who you personally enlist in the future. However, you have to work with the leaders you have in the meantime, and the ultimate aim is to get them on board with leading the Sunday school to be healthy and growing. You will need to meet regularly with your Sunday school leaders as a group to pray, plan, and equip. Gathering together will make a difference but personal relationships will require personal time. The investment admittedly requires a lot of time but will yield great results.

Call each and every Sunday school teacher at least once a month. You may talk about Sunday school but you don't have to. Talk about family, interests, and any other subject you would discuss with a friend. Share a one-on-one meal with every

Sunday school teacher every year. Invite a spouse along if the leader is of the opposite sex. New Sunday school directors and pastors will need to take many evening or lunch appointments early on to get a jump on this approach.

Seek out opportunities for leisure time in small groups over the course of time. Why is this important? The next time you introduce a new idea or make a key decision, the level of trust will be higher and you will receive less resistance. Relationships allow you to provide the leadership needed to strengthen the Sunday school.

Discuss scenarios in training sessions well in advance of implementation.

Interact with your leaders on potential subjects or sources of resistance while there is no pressure. Introduce scenarios such as those described in the "emergency" section of this chapter. In advance, discuss the merits of creating new classes, flexibility about room assignments, teacher training, teacher guidelines, and other subjects prone to resistance. Share the testimony of experts and the practices of healthy churches in approaching these issues. Also, take time to discuss responses to difficult classes and teachers.

The discussion serves several purposes. First, as you prepare the leaders for future implementation you are providing training. Second, you are setting a tone of teamwork by bringing leaders into a discussion of issues in advance of implementation. Third, you are maximizing buy-in of your teachers to your leadership and future implementation of ideas. Fourth, you are identifying the points of resistance in advance of any contention, which you then may be able to circumvent with the knowledge that you gain.

Raise expectations with improved training and standards.

Effective training is another long-term resolution to

minimizing resistance to healthy Sunday school practices. Gathering with Sunday school leaders to teach the "why" and the "how" can reduce fear, misunderstanding, and resistance. For example, you need to teach a session on why and how new classes should be created to all of your Sunday school teachers at least every twenty-four months. Do not assume that they know the why or the how. They love their group and enjoy great fellowship. Suppose that you have twelve Sunday school teachers and that you anticipate creating at least two new classes in the coming year. Why would you bother to plan an equipping session on creating new classes for all twelve teachers if only two of them will be affected next year? Because your aspiration is for all of them to be available in future years to assist in creating new classes, and by providing training and discussion in advance, you'll get them prepared for that eventuality.

What do your written guidelines say about cooperation? Take a moment to place your hands on the guidelines and underline the section on cooperation. Did you find it? It is possible to elevate the expectations of your leaders without being legalistic. You need to develop and communicate minimum standards and expectations for your leaders. Paul did this when he wrote to Timothy and suggested minimum standards for pastors, deacons, and their wives. He didn't include Sunday school teachers because that function emerged later in the history of the church! The leadership role of the Sunday school is critical to the health of a church, however. Uncommitted, untrained, or uncooperative Sunday school teachers will never be found leading a healthy, growing Sunday school ministry. Raising your expectations will of necessity require that you continue to improve the training and standards of your Sunday school leaders.

PART TWO

Common Class/Group Emergencies

CHAPTER 13

They Want to Split (or Change) My Class

✚ THE EMERGENCY

Greg has a real passion for teaching Sunday school. The adult class that he was assigned about three years ago really struggled. The attendance was always in the single digits when he began. Greg's devotion to the Lord, his desire to achieve, and a good combination of communication skills and relationship skills proved to be a great leadership blend. The class grew almost immediately under his leadership and is now by far the largest adult class in the church. The group has changed rooms twice to accommodate the growth. Greg loves his class, and the members have a great love for Greg and his wife, Leah.

Anyone can tell the class is great on the first visit. Almost thirty people attend the Bible study every Sunday morning. The class is well organized thanks to Leah's administrative gifts, and she has proven to be a great partner with Greg in leading the class. Every Sunday morning has the feel of celebration with warm fellowship and plenty of interaction. The members arrive early and greet guests warmly, and the Bible studies are getting better as the group grows and, just as importantly, as Greg grows. Guests are regularly invited, and rarely does a month go by without guests in attendance. The class has been blessed to see several people come to know Christ as Savior through their outreach.

Greg, however, received a huge shock last week and is now more discouraged than he has ever been since taking leadership of the class. The Sunday school director informed him that starting in the fall, just a few weeks away, a new class would be created, taking some of his members. "Why do they want to split our class?" he asked Leah when he broke the news to her. "We've grown this class, and our fellowship is second to none in our church. Why are we being punished for doing such a good job?" Greg is considering resigning because he feels insulted that the director wants to remove members from his class. "It just is not fair," he said as he complained about the situation to his group the following Sunday. The class members agreed, and several began to say privately that they would likely leave the church if Greg and Leah stepped down.

✚ TRIAGE

1. Do you believe that your pastor and Sunday school director have a sincere desire to lead the church to be faithful in fulfilling the Great Commission?

2. Would you be willing to release members of your group to serve or attend elsewhere if it would strengthen the church?

3. Have you communicated to your group that you will take no offense should they ever feel called to serve or attend another group, and have you given them release to do so?

4. Have you enlisted or released any members to serve outside of your group in the past twelve months?

5. Do you have a plan to grow and reproduce your group so that the leadership base can be expanded and more people can come to know Christ?

Diagnosis: Refer to page 17 to evaluate the severity of this emergency.

✢ PRESCRIPTION
Luke 5:6–7   Luke 10:2
1 Corinthians 3:6   Luke 9:1–2

✢ FIRST AID
Don't misinterpret a compliment as an insult.

Sunday school teachers sometimes get upset when a pastor or director approaches them about creating a new class. He or she often feels as if other leaders are seeking to tear down what they have worked so hard to build. Relationships have developed through the process and everything seems to be going so well. *Why do they want to split my class?*

Put yourself in the shoes of the director briefly and imagine that you see the need to create a new class. Where would you go for help? Would you seek out a teacher doing a poor job leading an unhealthy class? Would you want to duplicate a weak or dying class? Or would you seek out a healthy class with an effective teacher so that the new class would have a model to follow to improve the chances of its success? Starting a new class is challenging enough when support is provided and leaders have the right tools and experience.

Why were you approached to help launch a new group? You just received a pat on the back and your leaders have complimented your leadership. Why would you be upset with a compliment? Obviously, you have the admiration and respect of your leaders, and they want to replicate the kind of group that you have nurtured and developed. You should get more upset if you teach year after year and are not asked to help create a new class. Don't misinterpret the compliment you have received as an insult. Count your blessings!

No one desires to "split your class."

The term "split" is often used to describe what happens when a new class is created, but it is a poor choice of words. You will be asked to release some members to assist with the launch of the new class, whether it is to give up a couple to create a new preschool class or more than one couple to create a new adult class that is in a similar life stage to the one that you currently lead.

You need to remember a very important point if you lead an adult group. All current leaders reside in adult classes. The Sunday school cannot succeed if adult teachers are not intentional in developing and releasing leaders. If leaders are not provided by the existing adult classes, where will they come from? Recall that Jesus developed the apostles for three years and then released them to serve.

Creating a new class will not require that you give up half of your group or "split" your class. You are being asked to send forth one or more couples or members to create a new class in a similar way that the church should send forth missionaries. How would you characterize a church sending forth missionaries? Healthy or unhealthy? Apply that same thinking to your Sunday school class. Avoid selfish thinking. Thank God that He is using you to develop leaders to strengthen your congregation and to serve God's kingdom purposes.

See the big picture.

Creating a new class can be disruptive to your class and can be painful when all seems to be going so well with the group that you have. Creating classes is sometimes referred to as birthing a class. The analogy is appropriate since giving birth involves labor and pain. Ask a mom shortly after the birth of her child and she will tell you that the joy exceeds the pain very quickly. Could it be that the new class might reach someone with the good news that may have never been reached by an existing class? Would you be willing to sacrifice some members of your group to see someone born again? You may respond that there is no guarantee that anyone will come to Christ in the new class. You may be right. But, I absolutely guarantee you that no one will come to know Christ through the ministry of the new class if it is not created.

Creating new classes is essential to the health and growth of the Sunday school ministry. New classes will reach people that the existing groups may never reach. Creating a new class is similar to launching an additional boat onto a lake to fish. You can continue to fish from one boat, but you will likely catch more fish from two boats than one. A Sunday school cannot grow by twenty, thirty, or forty members with the existing classes. Thirty new members attending would mean that about sixty or more are enrolled and need to be ministered to. Can the classes that you have now minister and maintain contact with sixty or more people every week? You will need more classes, more teachers, and more leaders to reach out and minister to more people. Refusing to reach out to people is not an option.

Remember the concept of "follow the leader."

Did you ever play "follow the leader" when you were a child? Do you remember how the leader would walk under, over, and around obstacles while everyone was expected to do exactly as the leader did? The object of the game was to do exactly as the leader. As a leader, your attitude is critical. You can be assured that your class members will grumble and complain if that is what you do. Or, you can lead the class to rejoice that they have been complimented, and you can challenge them to assist you.

They will follow your lead. Seek to be a godly example in whatever issues and challenges you face as a Sunday school leader. Lead your class to face challenges with a Christlike spirit and keep a rein on your tone, even if you disagree.

✚ REHAB
Aspire to be a healthy class.

A healthy class is worth replicating, and the epitome of health is that it naturally reproduces itself. Is your class healthy? Would you rather be unhealthy? Perhaps you need a check-up and a long-term plan. A healthy class is characterized by these three qualities:

1. Lives are being changed. That will happen when people are studying God's Word and applying it to their daily lives. Obedience to the Word often requires changes in attitudes, actions, or priorities. James likens the Word of God to looking into a mirror (James 1:22–24). A person cannot obey unless he or she knows what to do. Lives are changed as you lead your members to study God's Word each week and to apply it to their lives. The Great Commission commands us to "make disciples" by "teaching them to obey all that I [Christ] have commanded you" (Matt. 28:19–20).

2. The lost are being reached. The result of lives being changed is a desire to share the message of the gospel so that others can experience the forgiveness and transformation that Christ has granted. "Go and make disciples of all nations, baptizing them," is the command of the Great Commission. Is your class working together to share the gospel with your community with a focus on the life stage that you are best acquainted with? If your class meets week after week without ever giving

attention to the lost community around you, then it is not healthy. As you sit and feed on the sweetness of God's Word each week, do not let your class grow fat and lazy. Lead them to get out of the class to provide fellowships, outreach, ministry, and a witness to their friends and neighbors. Lead your class to bear fruit by bringing others into a relationship with Christ.

3. Leaders are being released. Jesus said to make disciples of "all nations." You cannot keep everyone in one place and accomplish this task. Members will have to be stretched to accomplish this aim. Perhaps that is why Christ reminded His followers that "I am with you always, even to the end of the age." Send your members to serve. A healthy class develops and sends forth leaders. Your average attendance may not be any larger than it was a year ago, but you are exactly on target if you are sending forth leaders. Lead your class to understand that they exist primarily for Christ's employment rather than the group's enjoyment.

Aspire to reproduce and plan to bear fruit.

Make it your aim to reproduce your class at least once during your tenure as the Sunday school teacher. Can you envision your class launching two, three, or four classes and then those classes each launching one or more themselves? What a great blessing! Can you imagine how many people could come to faith in Christ, be touched, have their lives changed? Pray for it! Aspire to it. Plan to do it. When will your class launch a new class? Don't wait on your pastor or your director to suggest this. Begin praying and planning now to reproduce and bear fruit. May God bless you and may you see the fruit of what God can do when you get a kingdom vision and lead your class to bear fruit.

CHAPTER 14

We Never Have Any Guests

✚ THE EMERGENCY

Us Four and No More
By Steve Parr

The time has arrived, it is time to begin;
I sit here alone in my class once again,
But hope springs eternal in five minutes or so,
My first member arrives, I'm not totally alone.
We have conversation, and then through the door
Two more faithful members for our complement of four.
It's four every week, these three I've long known
We study God's Word, and close we have grown.
We've grown deeper each year, we laugh, we pray,
They can't split our class, we like it this way.
We've heard about outreach, contacts, and reaching,
But we shall let nothing interrupt my fine teaching.
We like how it is with our comfort and space,
We cushioned our chairs and painted our place.

Don't ask us to change, rearrange, or reach out,
We're fine how we are, of that there's no doubt.
We never have guests; it's no problem for us,
It's only our preacher and director who fuss.
It's us four, no more, and let it be known,
We're headed to heaven, but you're on your own.

✚ TRIAGE

1. Have any first-time guests been present in your class in the past four weeks?

2. Have any first-time guests been present in your class in the past three months?

3. Do you emphasize, track, and report total contacts made by your class each week?

4. Does your class participate in the church's outreach ministry? (If none exists, answer "no.")

5. Are you intentionally leading your class to be involved in outreach?

Diagnosis: Refer to page 17 to evaluate the severity of this emergency.

✚ PRESCRIPTION

Matthew 28:18–20   Matthew 9:37–38
Luke 15:1–7   Acts 1:8

✚ FIRST AID

Take a look in the mirror.

Looking into the mirror is the tough part of the solution. A class will not necessarily have guests each week—though that would be ideal—but why are there *never* any guests present?

Perhaps there are never any guests present in your church at all. The resolution to that problem may not be found in this chapter though much material in this book can assist in addressing the larger challenges. The difficulty in looking into the mirror is that you may have to confess that while other classes or groups have guests your class or group rarely or never does. What is different about your class?

Could it be that your class does not understand the purpose of the Sunday school ministry? Members will lack motivation for inviting guests if you or the class members suppose that the purpose is to study the Bible. Sunday school has a much broader purpose when viewed historically or theologically. A member need not invite guests to participate if the intention is simply personal Bible study. Members must be taught that the purpose of Sunday school is to engage them in the fulfillment of the Great Commission, which cannot be accomplished without them reaching out.

Could it be that your class has not been challenged to invite and bring guests? Where should the challenge come from? It must come from the leader of the class. If you are not motivating, modeling, challenging, teaching, and encouraging your members to be purposeful in inviting and bringing guests, you can expect that guests will rarely be present.

For the teacher looking in the mirror, here is the toughest question of all: Could it be that the members do not bring guests because the class is so boring? *Ouch!* You may wonder why the six, eight, or ten members that you do have show up if the class is so boring. Perhaps it is because they love you personally or have an abiding commitment to their involvement and to Christ. However, that may not obligate them in their own mind to invite or bring guests. How sad it would be if they failed to invite friends because they were concerned that the guests would never come back again. Are you a dynamic and growing teacher? You need not resign if you are not, but you must make a commitment to grow and improve. Otherwise you will continue to rarely or never have guests in your class.

See the fields.

"We don't have any prospects for our class." That cannot possibly be true. You may have only a few prospects; even if only one is available who does not know Christ, then your class has a mission to fulfill. Your group has several places from which to draw guests. If your church is in North America you are likely in a community where 60 to 90 percent of the population is unchurched. That does not mean that they go to another church but that they do not go to one at all and likely do not have a personal relationship with Christ.

Do the math for yourself. Take the population within ten miles of your church and multiply times .75. Many of those are in the same life stage represented by your class members. Though not every community has the same number of unchurched prospects, they all have one thing in common: unchurched people are present and need the ministry of your class and the message of Jesus Christ's saving grace.

Apply the law of large numbers.

The law of large numbers is easy to understand and is quickly applicable. Suppose that in the course of three months a class with ten attendees invites a total of one friend, never calls to check on absentees, and does not purposefully identify or pray for any unchurched prospects for their class.

By contrast, suppose that in that same three-month period a class in a church across town with about the same number of members invites a total of forty friends, calls every absentee every week (totaling about eighty additional contacts), and identifies and prays for twenty unchurched members in their same life stage. Which of these two classes is most likely to have a guest next Sunday? Which of the two best characterizes your class? Start applying the law of large numbers!

The needs of several different groups of people beg for the ministry and invitation of your class members:

- Unchurched members of the community or those who do not regularly attend any church

- Members of your church who are not connected to any Sunday school class

- People who are members of your class but never attend, come sporadically, or have dropped out

- People who would attend but cannot at this point because of temporary circumstances such as job responsibilities, illness, or personal crisis

Open the side doors.

You have some members of your community who have no interest in attending Sunday school or Bible study. However, they do enjoy camping, football, golf, theater, cookouts, skiing, music, parties, water polo, and about 389,403 other activities that are neither spiritual nor unspiritual in and of themselves.

Imagine that a neighbor has a bass fishing boat sitting in his garage. What would you think if he sat in his boat and fished in his garage? Unless his garage is literally next to the water, he wouldn't catch anything, right? The reality is that he must change his thinking. If the fish will not (or cannot) come to the boat, then he should take the boat to the fish.

Lead your class to purposefully engage in activities on weekends and holidays with the express purpose of inviting family, neighbors, and community members. While the activity will not guarantee that the guests will attend your Sunday school class, you may still minister, share the gospel, build relationships, and fellowship. You will find that members will often come to your class through the "side door" of an activity like this instead of through the front door of your church. Could that be why Jesus intentionally engaged in celebrations, meals, banquets, and activities in His community instead of exclusively teaching and ministering inside the synagogues? Open some side doors!

✚ REHAB
Lead your class to be evangelistic.

Evangelism takes intentionality. A Bible study group led by a teacher who remains silent about evangelism will not ordinarily take the initiative themselves. Evangelistic classes are led by evangelistic teachers. You may or may not be a skilled witness, but you can be a committed witness. Lead your class to take a team approach, together seeking opportunities to share the gospel.

As you read on page 167, many people have needs that merit ministry and invitations from your group to fellowships and Bible study. However, no need is as pressing as that of a person without a relationship with Christ. Make it the prayer and the aim of your class to see someone come to know Christ as Savior through the ministry and witness of your group within the year.

I discovered that three people trust Christ for every four classes in the denomination of which I am a member. You may discover the ratio is lower in the churches with which you are affiliated. Check it out in your own church. You will find that most churches would increase the number of baptisms if one person trusted Christ and was baptized for each class that exists. Teachers and classes that have an intentional evangelistic focus will find that guests are present frequently and, more importantly, that the class is blessed to see friends and family trusting Christ as Savior. Is your class evangelistic? You need to lead the way!

Work on the total environment.

Though churches are similar in many ways, they do not all have the same culture. The culture referenced at this point is not one of race, ethnicity, or nationality but a spiritual culture. Some churches are evangelistic and some are not. Some churches are assertive in outreach while others are not. Some emphasize openness to guests and some prefer to keep outsiders away. Practically every church considers their congregation to be friendly, but that is simply not true.

In some churches, people arrive early in anticipation of great things and then linger following the services, interacting and fellowshipping. In other churches, everyone arrives late and exits as quickly as possible following the final prayer. Do you have any doubt about which environment is more attractive to guests? James, in his second chapter, speaks about how the church should receive guests. Read and discover the climate of receptivity that he teaches the church to develop. The reason for developing a welcoming environment is to remove any obstacle that would hinder guests from hearing—and hopefully responding to—the gospel message. Surely you do not want unfriendliness, problems with facilities, or poor teaching to be a distraction.

Consider the following issues related to the environment of your class and endeavor to develop a culture that welcomes guests.

- Do the leaders and many of the members arrive early in order to prepare and welcome guests?

- Are the facilities clean, well kept, and free of clutter?

- Are the signs adequate to assist the guests in finding preschool facilities, restrooms, the worship area, Sunday school classrooms, etc.?

- Are people designated to serve as greeters to welcome and assist guests?

- Are name tags available in Sunday school classes for all participants to help the guests as well as members with names?

- Does the class have a plan to follow up with guests to express appreciation, initiate relationships, and invite them to return?

- Is the Bible study interactive, age-appropriate, and communicated with passion?

- Are fellowships planned to develop and strengthen relationships with members, recent guests, the unchurched, and prospective members?

Teach your class to "obey all that I [Christ] have commanded you."

"Go therefore and make disciples of all the nations, baptizing them in the name of the Father and of the Son, and of the Holy Spirit, teaching them to observe all that I have commanded you; and lo, I am with you always, even to the end of the age" (Matt. 28:19–20).

Leading your class members to grow deeper in their faith is commendable. Some leaders spiritualize their approach and use this mind-set as an excuse to avoid outreach. The Great Commission was spoken by Jesus as He prepared to ascend to be with the Father. His final words to the apostles were preserved in Holy Scripture and are as relevant to believers as if He were standing face to face summarizing His instructions to all of His followers. You will notice that He commanded them to "observe all that" he had taught them.

Did Jesus teach that believers should reach out to the lost, the unchurched, and the hurting? He not only taught it but also modeled it throughout His ministry. Outreach is not a suggestion or one of the options that a leader or a class might want to consider. Reaching out to those without Christ is not the whole of the believer's existence but is encompassed in what Jesus did and taught in the Gospels and throughout the New Testament. Having guests in a Sunday school class should be a typical occurrence because obedience to the Great Commission itself should inspire every leader and every group to be intentional in growing in their faith, obeying all that Christ commanded, and working together to reach out to the community and ultimately to the world. Be diligent to teach "all that Christ commanded," including evangelism and outreach to the unchurched.

CHAPTER 15

Our Guests Never Return

✚ THE EMERGENCY

Michelle and J.R. recently relocated thanks to a great job opportunity that was sure to advance J.R.'s career. They were both anxious and excited about their new adventure as they loaded up their two small children and moved several hours from the familiar surroundings they had known all of their lives.

The move represented a fresh start for them in many ways, and they had discussed a desire to reconnect to church after several years of absence. J.R. was once a faithful member of his home church but had wavered in his faith since his college days. He was confident in his relationship with Christ but had gotten detoured and distracted for several years. He was convicted of his need to recommit and to grow in his faith again. Michelle had attended church occasionally growing up but could not say that she had a relationship with Christ. However, she had thought about faith often since the children came along and wanted to know more. She and J.R. agreed that the children needed spiritual roots and that finding a church home would be a priority as soon as the move was complete.

Michelle drove by a church within a couple of days that

was close to their new home and was affiliated with a denomination to which they both had agreed would reflect their convictions and preferences. Michelle did not know if there was much difference at this point but relied on the experience of her husband in making that choice. She noted that Sunday school started at 9:45 a.m. followed by worship services at 11 a.m. according the sign in front of the church. J.R. and Michelle agreed that jumping in feet first would be just what the children needed in order to make friends quickly, so they decided to go to Sunday school on the first visit.

A hectic morning of getting the kids ready did not deter J.R. and Michelle, and they arrived about ten minutes early to find their way around. They were surprised to find the parking lot virtually empty. After double checking the clock and the church sign, assured that the timing was correct, they made their way in and passed two ladies who gave them a strange look and offered no word of greeting or assistance. They wandered for several minutes before accidentally stumbling into the children's area. While decorated appropriately, there was one thing glaringly absent: no one was there. They stood there for a few minutes before a gentlemen noticed them and came by to assist. "I am sorry," he exclaimed, "the teacher will be here shortly." He explained that the children were all combined in one class due to the fact that so few attended the church.

Michelle uneasily parted with her children, Jessica and Emma, once the teacher arrived. Michelle began to surmise that the church did not have its act together, and wondered about the qualifications of the person with whom she had left them. Upon being escorted to their own Sunday school class, they received yet another surprise. As the members arrived they felt as if they were in the wrong place. The sign on the door stated the class was for young couples, but no one in the class other than J.R. and Michelle could have been under age fifty. J.R. whispered to Michelle, "If these are the young couples, the senior couples must all be over ninety!" They quickly discovered they had little in common with these folks, but it did not seem to matter much after all. Aside from a half-hearted greeting, no one really engaged them in any significant conversation anyway. At least they had the Bible study to look forward to . . . or so they thought.

Following prayer requests that covered every ailment known to man, the teacher proceeded to pretty much read the lesson to the class. To make matters worse, he didn't even read it that well. The visit turned out to be a total waste of time. J.R. could not remember a longer hour in his life. Unfortunately, the worship experience mirrored that of the Sunday school hour. Sadly, instead of excitement, J.R. and Michelle felt relief to have it over with. *Maybe church is just not for our family*, Michelle thought. *Church isn't what it used to be*, went through J.R.'s mind. "Dad, do we have to go back?" Emma asked. They did not go back, nor did they bother to visit anywhere else. The members of the church never even noticed.

✝ TRIAGE

1. Has the class enrolled anyone new in the past two months?

2. Do members of the class arrive early to fellowship and welcome guests?

3. Does the class have an intentional plan to follow up with guests?

4. Is the Bible study well prepared, interactive, and delivered with passion?

5. Is the congregation and church leadership intentional in providing an environment that is welcoming to guests?

Diagnosis: Refer to page 17 to evaluate the severity of this emergency.

✚ PRESCRIPTION
James 2:1–9
Acts 2:47
1 Peter 4:9–10

✚ FIRST AID
Take a look into the mirror, again.

The first step in addressing this problem is the same as in the preceding issue of a class that never has any guests. The circumstance described here is mildly less troubling because guests are attending. However, the net result is the same. You do indeed have a problem if guests are attending but none ever return or join.

Of course, not all guests are expected to return. Guests visiting your group do so for a variety of reasons. Some may be from out of town and have chosen to attend with family or friends. Others may be members of other local churches, again having chosen to attend with family or friends, with no intention of being present more than once.

You can expect, however, when several guests visit over the course of a few months that many will be unchurched and that their visit is an opportunity to connect them to the body of believers and to share the gospel. If none of those guests ever return, you will need to take a look into the mirror and conduct an honest evaluation.

Begin the evaluation by having a discussion with your class or group. Boldly put this issue on the table and discuss class, congregational, and teacher dynamics. What is the spirit like in the class itself when you meet each week? Do leaders and members arrive early to prepare and make guests feel welcome? Is there a sense of expectation and excitement about the class? Are group members friendly to newcomers and intentional in connecting with them on a personal level? Does the class follow up by contacting and expressing gratitude? Are the guests invited to fellowship opportunities to get to know members better?

Why would a guest want to return to your class? Is the teaching interesting? Bible centered? Relevant? Well-prepared? Age-appropriate? Interactive? Does the church have well-kept facilities? Quality childcare? Guest-friendly signs? These are tough questions, and the answers can sting. However, the class must take a reality check and make adjustments. God forbid that one of the guests who doesn't know Christ does not feel welcomed or feel that the visit was worth their time, or that the guest does not have occasion to hear and respond to the gospel.

Dig deeper into the issues by getting objective evaluation. You can accomplish this task by enlisting an anonymous guest to visit and follow up with an evaluation of the experience. You may also accomplish the task by calling and debriefing those who have visited. Contact the last ten guests to the class and ask them to provide straightforward evaluation. The answers they give may enable the group to see shortcomings and areas that need attention.

Looking into the mirror can be painful when the reflection is less than that to which we aspire. But the guests that God blesses the class with and the message of the gospel are too valuable to be buried beneath a fear of acknowledging your strengths and weaknesses. Addressing the flaws that are discovered is one way to commit to God a willingness to do whatever necessary to effectively represent Christ as members of His body.

Initiate a follow-up plan.

Suppose that a guest attends your class next Sunday. Make a numbered list of all the things that will automatically happen to that guest on behalf of the class in the next thirty days. Do not place anything on the list that is not 100 percent guaranteed to happen. Here are two examples: First, the guest will be invited to go to lunch that afternoon by one or more of our members. Second, the guest will get a call from one of the class members on Monday evening. Go ahead and make your list now . . .

What did you come up with? Perhaps you could not come up with anything that was automatic. Maybe you came up with one or two items but in reality had to exaggerate the likelihood that it would happen. You may have identified part of the problem.

Lead a discussion with your group and develop a list of five to ten ways to touch the life of every guest who visits your class. I hesitate to include a list because it is so important for your class to go through this exercise and to customize a process appropriate to the life stage of your group and the community in which you live. Consider the following only as an example:

1. At least two greeters will be present each week, excluding the teacher or group leader, at least fifteen minutes early to receive and welcome guests (and members).

2. Name tags will be provided each week to members and guests to enhance personal interaction.

3. The members/couples sitting closest to the guests are responsible for extending an invitation to sit together in worship.

4. On a rotating basis, members will be assigned to invite the guests to lunch. If they are not available the members will make effort to connect later in the week or as soon as possible to share a meal together.

5. The teacher will call all guests on Sunday afternoon. Upon determining that the guest lives in the community and does not regularly attend another church, he or she

will be asked permission to be added to the class roster or roll in order to be prayed for each week, invited to fellowships, ministered to by the class, and to attend Bible study when possible.

6. The person(s) that the guest attended with will go to the home of the guest within forty-eight hours to express appreciation for the visit. Or, for guests not connected to a class member, this can be done by class members on a rotating basis.

7. Guests' names will be placed on a roster or prospect list to be invited to all class fellowships for the next twelve months.

✛ REHAB
Become a climatologist.

What is the climate of your class like? I grew up in the northern part of Georgia. My mom always loved to plant flowers and to make the landscaping of our home look inviting. She once planted a banana tree in our backyard that would be moved to our basement during the coldest part of the year and then replanted each spring. The climate of north Georgia is anything but tropical—not conducive for a banana tree. It did live, mind you, but it never produced any fruit. Your class is certainly alive, because members are there every week, but is it producing any fruit? If guests are never returning you must evaluate the climate.

During the course of the first-aid section, you invested time in evaluating by looking into the mirror. Perhaps you discovered that the class does not have *a* flaw but has *many* flaws. Those flaws are affecting the climate of the class. Some people think that Sunday school is boring; the person with this mindset has had an experience that shaded his or her view of Sunday school.

Improvement of the climate will require that you invest time improving the following in this priority order:

1. The spiritual climate (Acts 4:31)

2. The teaching (2 Tim. 4:1–5)

3. The way guests are received, welcomed, and followed up with (James 2:1–9)

4. Relationship building and fellowship (Acts 2:42–47)

5. The physical environment (*Note*: Though it will not keep, it can repulse.)

Become more purposeful in relationship building.
You have already begun to take some steps to address this concern if you have applied what has previously been shared. At this point you should consider three relationship building essentials. Guests will sometimes attend with friends, and in that case, relationship building may happen more spontaneously. But you cannot assume that a relationship will develop; if you do, you will continue to fail to have guests return. Even those guests who return for a subsequent visit will not connect or join unless they develop a relationship with someone in the group. Give purposeful and persistent attention to these three phases:

1. The class must interact with the guest(s) on a personal level during the initial visit. You have to strike a balance between making them feel welcomed and at the same time making them feel as if they already belong. Avoid doing anything that would potentially embarrass them such as calling on them to pray, read, stand up in front of everyone, interrogating them, or ignoring them. You might make them feel

a bit more at ease by having everyone provide a brief introduction, members and guests alike. Keep in mind that the
few minutes before the class and the few minutes after are
equally important to what happens when the Bible study is
going on.

2. Make contact within the next two days. The contact needs
   to be personal—either by phone, a personal visit, or sharing
   a meal with a class member. You will lose momentum if
   you wait two or three weeks. The fact that they visited the
   class is an indication of interest and that God is at work
   right now. You might also discover quickly that they belong to another congregation or that they are from out of
   town. You can express appreciation at that point without
   investing an inappropriate amount of energy pursuing the
   follow-up.

3. A member or couple of the class must begin to spend time
   with the recent guest outside of the Bible study setting. The
   relationship takes a giant leap forward when this happens
   and the possibility of future visits, openness to the gospel,
   and potential membership increases dramatically when
   this happens. You must be intentional in connecting them
   to the community of your class and that will happen only if
   one or more relationships are developed.

Maintain contact and ministry.

How long do you continue follow-up? You certainly may
discontinue if you discover that guests regularly attend another
church or if they do not live in your community and therefore
will not be returning. However, you may still have future opportunities to connect with them if the class maintains contact.
The frequency of the contact will lessen, but you will want to
continue with two practices for at least a year.

1. Contact and invite them to attend your class fellowships. Attendance at a class gathering or party on a weekend in future months may present an additional opportunity to develop a relationship that will connect the previous guest to the group.

2. Maintain contact by phone at least monthly seeking to discover prayer requests. The requests that are received may alert the group to a ministry opportunity if a crisis of some nature is discovered. Significant outreach and ministry during a time of crisis is often a turning point in establishing appreciation, building relationships, and encouraging a previous guest to consider the value of being connected to a group that ministers with diligence and compassion.

Do not assume because a guest does not return or does not initially respond that he or she will never return. Maintain prayerful contact and diligent ministry and some guests may connect at a future point.

CHAPTER 16

No One Wants to Help with Outreach

✚ THE EMERGENCY

"He who thinks he leadeth and has no one following is only taking a walk." —John Maxwell

"Leadership is getting men to do what they really do not want to do in order to accomplish what they really do want to accomplish." —Tom Landry

"We were lost, but we were making good time." —Yogi Berra

You have your hands full as a Sunday school teacher with responsibilities for lesson preparation, presentation, and leading the class in fellowship, ministry, outreach, and follow-up of guests. In addition, you likely have other church responsibilities on top of home obligations and work demands. With so many expectations, it is easy to let outreach slide. However, obedience to the Great Commission compels Christian leaders to keep those under their care devoted to outreach.

Outreach? Outreach involves leading your group to purposefully give attention to those who do not know Christ as Savior and to believers not connected to the body of Christ in order to lead others into a growing relationship with Jesus. The Great Commission characterizes that process as "making disciples."

Have you noticed that believers often want to do anything and everything other than outreach? Outreach and evangelism efforts are conducted not only in obedience to the Great Commission but also on the premise that a relationship with Jesus Christ is the only way to heaven and that those who do not trust Christ as Savior spend eternity separated from God bearing punishment for their sins. It is not a pretty picture. God has not commanded you to save anyone, but He clearly compels you to sow the seeds of the gospel, inviting others to come into a relationship with Him.

You are in a spiritual battle. Satan will do all within his power to keep you and the members of your group from doing anything that will spread the gospel. Do not let him have any victory over you or your class in this regard. You must lead your group to do outreach. It will not be easy and some may never get on board. Remember that the Great Commission is not the Great Suggestion, and determine to engage your class in conducting outreach.

✚ TRIAGE

1. Teacher: Are you an evangelistic leader?

2. Does the class have an outreach leader or someone with similar responsibilities?

3. Does the class often have discussions about outreach?

4. Do you enlist directly rather than by announcement to the whole group?

5. Does the class regularly pray by name for those who do not know Christ?

Diagnosis: Refer to page 17 to evaluate the severity of this emergency.

✦ PRESCRIPTION
Matthew 28:18–20
Ephesians 4:15b–16
Luke 15:1–7

✦ FIRST AID
Begin at the beginning.
You must begin with the leader of the group. That is you. You lead the way for your group in setting the agenda, the priorities, and the activities of the group. You have your own gifts, passions, and even opinions about the purpose for your group. Perhaps you fall in the majority of those who propose that the purpose of Sunday school is Bible study. Perhaps you are like many teachers who just want to teach. What are you to teach? You find the instruction in the Great Commission.

The instruction is not to teach some of what God commanded or to teach the portions of His commands that we prefer. You are to be "teaching them to observe all things that I [Christ] have commanded you" (Matt. 28:20a). You cannot do that without leading your class to be involved in outreach. The question is not "Should I do it?" or "Do I have time to do it?" but "How am I going to do it?" You must teach your group to be obedient to Christ's command. That requires specific action.

You have probably noticed that while your group members will do almost anything else, they tend to be resistant to outreach. That is why they need a leader like you, and that is why God has placed you in the group. Have you ever wondered why people are so resistant to evangelism and outreach? If a member or a couple in your group won six free tickets to the Super Bowl, would they take their two and discard the other four? If they won ten tickets to Broadway along with free airfare and hotel, would they take their tickets and keep the other eight a secret? And yet they have eternal life and know that it is freely available by God's grace to others and do not want to be involved in sharing it with others. *What is going on?* Your class is engaged in a spiritual battle where the enemy deceives and distracts in every way possible to keep them from sharing the Good News. Stand up. You are the leader of the group. It is time to get the group engaged in outreach.

Begin praying for the lost.

Your group regularly shares prayer requests with one another. One of the great benefits of belonging to a small group of believers is the opportunity to support one another in prayer through the difficulties of life whether great or small. The group prays not only for one another but also for missionaries, civic leaders, families, pastors, communities, and for any and every need placed upon the heart of a member. The largest group your class prays for is ordinarily those who are experiencing sickness. Each request is submitted in sincerity, and all are worthy of the group's attention.

In addition, the prayer requests inform the class of how they can minister to the members and to those outside the group when requests are verbalized each week. The sharing of personal prayer requests binds the group together and deepens relationships as personal needs are shared. The group not only prays but also empathizes when a member shares of a crisis in the family or in their personal lives. Every prayer request merits the attention of the group.

As you think about the value of the prayer ministry of your group, consider:

- Is there anything more severe than for a person to die in their sin without the blessing of experiencing the forgiveness and salvation offered by the sacrificial death and resurrection of the Lord Jesus Christ?

- Do you believe that those who die in their sin are eternally separated from God and suffer eternal punishment?

Do you remember when Christ illustrated the severity of this circumstance by stating,

> "If your right eye causes you to sin, pluck it out and cast it from you; for it is more profitable for you that one of your members perish, than for your whole body to be cast into hell. And if your right hand causes you to sin, cut it off and cast it from you; for it is more profitable for you that one of your members perish, than for your whole body to be cast into hell. (Matt. 5:29–30)

None of the crises your group prays for are as severe as the need of those who might die without a personal relationship with Jesus. I am not suggesting that we should not pray for one another's needs, but I am proposing that failing to pray for the lost is a tragic oversight if we really believe that Jesus is the author of salvation. The very least a group can do in engaging in outreach is to pray for the salvation of those who do not have a relationship with Christ. Begin this week: have your class make a list of family and friends in the community who do not clearly have a relationship with Jesus Christ and begin praying for them. A study that I conducted of Georgia's top evangelistic churches revealed that the most effective churches pray for the lost by name.[1] Prayer not only affects those who are the recipients but also the group as they are reminded and encouraged to minister and to be a witness to those in need of salvation. Lead your class to begin praying for the lost and unchurched by name.

Enlist the proper way.

"I cannot get anyone to help me!" How was it that Jesus enlisted the apostles? Did He make a public announcement and ask people to sign up if interested? No. According to Luke 6:12, He prayed all night. As you study the New Testament account you will discover that He went and directly invited the apostles to follow Him.

Begin by praying about who should be the outreach leader for your class. Ask God to show you. Once He does you need to ask to meet with that person privately (not beside the welcome center in the hallway) or with you and your spouse or another group member if the person is of the opposite sex. Tell the individual that God has placed something on your heart that you want to share. When you meet, you should share what you have been praying about and what God has placed on your heart. Share two or three things that you need from an outreach leader (or whatever the role) and how long the commitment will be. You do not want an immediate answer; ask the individual to pray about helping in this area, and indicate that you will check back in a few days.

You will get one of three responses from the people you ask: (1) The individual will likely say yes, and you will have your leader. (2) The individual may say no, and you must trust that God either will deal with the disobedience or that He is leading

---

1. Steve R. Parr, Georgia Baptist Convention, "Georgia's Top Evangelistic Churches: Ten Lessons from the Most Effective Churches" (2008), 10–11, http://gabaptist.org/FAITHNETWORK_UserFileStore/fileCabinet/ministries/237e6518-ae1d-4db3-844a-2959aa6966fc/em_Ga_Top_Evangelistic_Churches_bk.pdf.

in some other way. You have complimented the individual by asking, and God may be purposefully using your encouragement. (3) The individual may respond that he or she is not comfortable with outreach but wonder if there is some other way to help. That would be a blessing. The person might not have served at all had you not suggested the role of outreach leader. Enlisting directly in this manner is more time-consuming, but you will get better results because it is based in prayer and engages the Holy Spirit in the enlistment process.

✚ REHAB
Elevate outreach.

Your group will not be likely to provide the assistance that you need with outreach unless you make outreach one of the priorities of your class. Josh Hunt conducted research that revealed two great benefits for a group that keeps the focus on outreach. The first benefit is perhaps obvious, but the second may surprise you. Hunt surveyed more than 1,000 Sunday school leaders and asked if they saw their primary purpose as spiritual growth or outreach. Groups who saw their primary purpose as being more about reaching others outside the group than growing spiritually were 53 percent more likely to be growing than those groups who saw their primary purpose as growing spiritually.[2]

The first result makes perfect sense but here comes the surprise. He further discovered that groups that saw their purpose as primarily about reaching out to others were exactly twice as likely to report the highest levels of spiritual vibrancy, compared with those who saw their primary purpose as spiritual growth.[3] Do you understand why that is? Spiritual growth is not about learning but about learning and applying. Jesus instructed His

---

2. Josh Hunt, *Make Your Group Grow: Simple Stuff That Really Works* (Loveland, CO: Group Publishing, 2010), 24.
3. Ibid.

disciples but is seen throughout the Gospels leading them into the community to reach out and to minister. A Sunday school with a Great Commission focus is not a place to gather but a rallying place to launch from in an effort to touch lives. Here are five ways you can continue to elevate outreach in your group throughout the year:

1. Personally enlist someone to serve with you to assist with keeping an outreach focus.

2. Lead the class to identify and pray weekly for family, friends, and acquaintances who do not clearly have a personal relationship with Christ.

3. Plan several fellowships over the next year with consideration for what will attract the participation of guests and unchurched friends who are invited by members. Be purposeful in planning well, inviting lots of guests, and sharing the testimony of one of the members so that the gospel can be shared.

4. Spend five minutes each week discussing outreach ideas and challenges with your group prior to Bible study.

5. Engage your class in inviting members to attend Sunday school, worship, and fellowships. Guests come when they are invited. Teach your group the law of large numbers. A few invitations may result in guests attending but many invitations will guarantee it. Lead the class to invite dozens to each fellowship and to the Bible study each month.

Participate in existing outreach opportunities.

The final long-term principle is simple and almost

self-explanatory. What is already being offered in your church to assist and challenge the group in conducting outreach? Does your church have an organized visitation and outreach night? If so, get your group involved. Remember that it begins with you. Make a commitment to participate and personally enlist someone to attend with you. Is your church providing personal evangelism training in the coming months? Personally enlist members of your group to participate. Is your church hosting an event or ministry with an outreach focus such as vacation Bible school, an evangelistic revival, or a men's or women's banquet? Involve your class in inviting and bringing the un-churched to participate. Do not wait on your church to provide outreach opportunities in order for your group to be outreach focused and do not miss opportunities that are being provided by your pastor or staff that will enhance the outreach effectiveness of your group.

CHAPTER 17

I Cannot Get Anyone Involved in Discussion

✚ THE EMERGENCY

Have you ever raised your hand during the worship service? People sometimes raise their hands as a display of adoration, praise, worship, or agreement with the message being presented. That is all well and good, but it is not what I am referring to. Have you ever raised your hand to ask a question during the worship service? The pastor is well into his sermon and making a well-prepared and executed point when suddenly your hand goes up. What does the pastor do at that point? I will tell you what he does. He keeps on preaching his message. As a matter of fact, he may preach with even more enthusiasm thinking that you are raising your hand in praise or agreement.

An audience of dozens or even hundreds of people does not lend itself to a good opportunity to raise one's hand and ask questions. The reasons are not spiritual or unreasonable but practical. However, people do have questions sometimes. A person in the audience may have a thought, an experience, a concern, a testimony, or a desire for clarification on some point made by the pastor. Asking questions, interacting, and even debating can serve as valuable components of the learning and growth process. Every believer needs the opportunity to have such interaction in order to maximize personal growth. Meeting regularly with a small group apart from the large group worship experience provides a venue for that need to be met. Jesus called out twelve whom He named apostles and interacted and led them to a depth of growth that was not possible with a large crowd.

You do not have to be convinced of this principle. You lead a Sunday school class and meet with a small group every week. They can raise their hands, ask their questions, and share their thoughts. But—would you believe it?—some groups will not talk or interact during the Bible study. The group just sits in their seats and refuses to participate. What do you do when no one will participate in discussion?

✚ TRIAGE

1. Have you participated in training for Sunday school leaders?

2. Is lecture your primary method of teaching?

3. Do you sometimes subdivide your class into smaller groups for discussion?

4. Do you intentionally utilize multiple methods in your teaching?

5. Would your group members consider you to be a passionate teacher?

Diagnosis: Refer to page 17 to evaluate the severity of this emergency.

✚ PRESCRIPTION
Mark 4:10–13
Luke 6:12–16
Matthew 16:13–16

✚ FIRST AID
Spend time on relationships.

Consider an occasion when you sat with a friend over a meal or in your home. Recall how you interacted and conversed for perhaps hours. The time likely went quickly with little lapse in the conversation. Good relationships lead to good conversations. What about your group? Is the group new or has it been together for several months? The beginning stages of a group can be awkward prior to the development of relationships. The concern that you should have over lack of participation in discussion is greater if the group has been together for a longer period of time.

Begin relationship building by asking questions prior to diving into Bible study. Help the group in getting to know one another. A nonthreatening warm-up question can help in getting the group accustomed to sharing and will enhance relationships as members discover more about one another.

- What is your favorite wintertime leisure activity?

- What was the first car that you ever owned?

- Where would you go for a dream vacation?

- As a child, what did you want to be when you grew up?

These elementary questions may appear to lack any spiritual purpose. However, the answers will reveal the backgrounds, preferences, experiences, and personalities of the members.

Relationships mature as the group knows more about each of the other members.

You can fast forward relationship building with fellowship activities that take place apart from the formal Bible study gathering time. Initiate opportunities when the group can spend leisure time together in informal settings. Although the group's fellowships should reach out to the unchurched, in the early stages of group life you should urge relationship development among the group members.

Don't fear temporary silence.

You have asked the group a question with the hope that a response might lead to discussion. Ten seconds go by and then twenty. Twenty seconds seems like several minutes. The silence is awkward, and the fear that no one will step up causes you to come to your own rescue. You jump back in and share the solution or move on to your next point. Though it's not your intention, your response may be hindering further discussion. When you do answer your own question you are signaling to the group that their input is not required. When you are willing to allow the silence to continue, though awkward, you are signaling that interaction is expected. Do not be afraid of silence, and do not be too quick to come to the rescue. However, if the seconds begin to turn to tens of seconds, consider the next steps.

Rephrase the question.

If the silence continues you may need to ask the question again. However, consider the possibility that the group either did not understand the original question or that the question was poorly presented. Is the point of the question to encourage discussion? If so, be sure that the question that you present is open-ended. If the question is factual, it could be that no one knows the answer, or that they are uncertain and perhaps fear being corrected. Conversely, perhaps everyone knows the answer and would feel foolish answering something so obvious. An open-ended question is concerned with feelings, opinions, experiences, and perspectives.

What do you do if the question is open-ended and still there is no response? You might urge reaction by asking what the general consensus of a group would be to the particular issue. How would most Christians respond to the question? How would most people in our community respond to the question? How would most unchurched people respond to the question? Providing this option permits a response while minimizing fear because it is a reaction to the common opinions of others. You can follow by asking for the group to share ways that the previous responses concur with or contradict a biblical view of the issue.

Subdivide the group.

Some people will never raise their hand or offer a response or opinion in a group. The same people will talk incessantly when they are one-on-one. Other people may blend in to a group of twenty but take leadership in a group of five. The bottom line is that the smaller the group the higher the likelihood of inter-action between all members of the group. Therefore, you may need to subdivide the group occasionally to encourage discussion. It is a simple process and can be done spontaneously.

Perhaps you have gone through awkward silence or people are just not responding. Ask the members to divide into smaller groups of no fewer than three and no more than four. You can use smaller numbers for smaller groups and larger numbers for larger groups, but keep them between two and five. Pose the question and ask the group to take two to three minutes to discuss. You may ask them to share their personal thoughts or to come to a consensus about the commonly held opinions of others as previously described. Follow by asking for volunteers to share a quick summary of the individual group responses and facilitate further discussion as time permits.

✚ REHAB
Master multiple methods.

Jesus was a master teacher. He understood that those He created were all unique and that the way in which they best learned varied from person to person. Did Jesus ever lecture? Yes He did, as you can observe in a study of the Sermon on the Mount in Matthew 5–7. Did He ever utilize any other methods? Absolutely! He used word pictures, storytelling, object lessons, drama, debate, question and answer, examples, and hands-on experiences, just to name a few. Why did He not simply lecture all of the time as He taught? The different methods were used to capture the attention of different people and to reinforce what was being taught.

Sunday school leaders sometimes feature lecture as a primary method and may be inadvertently hindering interaction and discussion. A wise leader will do well to follow the example of the Master Teacher. Implementation of multiple, well-prepared teaching methods will encourage greater participation and less passivity during the course of the Bible study time. Take every possible opportunity to read books and materials that enhance your skills in Bible study presentation and age-appropriate methods. Make participation in training opportunities provided by your church leaders a priority in order to take full advantage of your own growth opportunities. Though giftedness plays a role in your teaching abilities it will be the development of skills that helps you to become a teacher who engages the group in order to urge their personal growth and to effectively make disciples.

CHAPTER 18

My Class Has No Life (or Lacks Morale)

✚ THE EMERGENCY

- Boring
- A waste of time
- Not worth my time
- Uninspiring
- A burden
- Irrelevant
- A drag
- Useless

Can you imagine the apostles saying any of that about spending time together with Jesus? You can be assured that the apostles did not lack life because they connected themselves to "the resurrection and the life," which was Jesus. What words or phrases would your group members use to describe your weekly gatherings?

You may think that "Sunday school is the problem" and that "it just does not work," but you would be wrong. Many groups are meeting every week to engage in inspirational Bible study, enjoyable fellowship, and purposeful outreach to the unchurched. You will never find a place in Scripture where the apostles complained about having to meet in a small group. On the contrary, they looked forward to small group gatherings.

What are your group members thinking? What do you want them to say about your group? What would Christ want them to say about life in your group?

- Enjoyable
- Motivational
- Meaningful
- Challenging
- Passionate
- Essential
- Highlight of my week
- Helps me grow in my faith

If your group is lacking life or morale, you cannot let that stand. You must take action and lead your group to be what God desires them to be.

✚ TRIAGE

1. Are you passionate about teaching?

2. Are you excited about what God is going to do through your group in the coming months?

3. Do you spend a great amount of time in prayer for your group?

4. Are you leading your group as well as teaching them?

5. Are you intentional in preparing and leading your group to reach others?

Diagnosis: Refer to page 17 to evaluate the severity of this emergency.

✚ PRESCRIPTION
Acts 4:31
Colossians 3:23
Acts 2:41–47

✚ FIRST AID
Vision is more than a buzz word.

Are you excited about your group? Are you excited about what God is going to do in them and through them in the coming year? Have you expressed to all members and prospective members of your group that you are excited about your class? If you are not excited about your group then why should they be? It is not enough to just be excited about the group. What is your vision for the group? What do you see God doing with them in the coming year? Where are you leading the group to go?

The reason many groups lack life is because the leader lacks life. Perhaps you are in your role because no one else would do it. Buckle up, my friend. You are not in your leadership role by accident. God not only saw it coming but knew that you would be the person leading the group. The solution for you as the leader is not to step down but to step up and do what God has called you to do. What does He want to do with your group? That is the vision. You have been called, by God, to lead the group to move in the direction of God's vision or desire for the group. Should that be boring, irrelevant, or uninspiring? I think not. *Vision* is not a buzz word. The Scripture teaches that "where there is no vision, the people perish" (Prov. 29:18a KJV). Seek the vision. Share the vision. Keep the vision in front of your group continually and work together to move toward it.

And when they had prayed . . .

Acts 4:31 is a powerful verse and an applicable prescription for a class that is lacking life or morale: "And when they had prayed, the place where they were assembled together was shaken; and they were all filled with the Holy Spirit, and they spoke the word of God with boldness." Did you notice the results of their actions? The place was shaken! That is what needs to happen to your group if it lacks life. They were all filled with the Spirit and witnessed boldly. What was the action that preceded these results? The Scripture says that these things happened "when they had prayed."

Are you praying for your group? Is your group praying together? I am not speaking of a sweet little prayer but a desperate seeking of God to do something with your group. I am speaking of praying in the manner of Jacob who grabbed hold of the angel and said, "I will not let You go unless You bless me!" (Gen. 32:26a). Are you really desperately, consistently, passionately praying? Get to it!

You are called to lead.

Your title is likely that of Sunday school teacher though it is understood that some small groups use other designations. You meet with your group to teach a Bible study each week. How is that working for you? If your group is lacking life then something is missing. You can teach your group every week while providing little or no leadership. However, a group that is lacking life needs leadership. Yes, they need God to work and they need the power of the Spirit, but they are stuck in a lifeless state and someone needs to lead them out.

Leadership is not a word to be feared by believers. It is implied when Jesus says that His followers are to be salt and light (Matt. 5:13–16). Salt is used to influence the flavor of the food you eat. Light has an influence over darkness. You do not put a light under a basket or use salt that has lost its flavor because the influence is negated. You are to develop and utilize your skills in spiritual leadership to influence your group to move them from where they are to where they need to be. The vision discussed earlier reflects where they need to be. The current reality reflects where they are now. You are called to develop the steps and take them through a process that moves them month by month closer to where they need to be. Your teaching will be a critical component of that process. However, every Sunday school class in the world would be thriving if simply teaching a Bible lesson every week were the whole of the process. It is time to step forward and lead.

✚ REHAB
You have to keep growing.

Perhaps you are experiencing some conviction because you are lacking in your personal leadership skills. You may be surprised at how your deficiencies place you in a unique position to be used by God. If you are willing to admit and confront your weaknesses and allow God to develop you as a leader then He will get the glory. Some people are natural leaders but you can take heart that much about leadership can be learned. You may or may not have the capacity to be as great of a leader as that person whom you admire and place on a pedestal, but the reality is that you can develop and improve your leadership skills.

Effective leadership of your group requires that you continually grow in two areas. The first is the most obvious: you must seek to grow spiritually. Growing in your relationship with Christ fuels your passion. That passion will often in turn be an inspiration to others and can attract them to your leadership. Though it has a practical effect it is the personal effect that is most important. You cannot take people where you have not been yourself or where you are not willing to go. Does your group see the growth occurring in you? Are you growing closer to Christ? Growth comes as a result of prayer, worship, and the study of God's Word. Failure in these areas will result in a forfeit of your credibility as a spiritual leader.

Second, you also must seek to grow in your leadership skills. The ability to influence and motivate followers is affected by your spiritual growth and passion but also includes practical skills such as understanding how to motivate, how to manage your time, how to enlist leaders, how to equip leaders, how to work with volunteers, and how to organize your group. These skills and others have practical components that can help you in your leadership effectiveness. They are learned by intentionally developing your leadership skills through the observation of effective leaders, receiving mentoring or coaching, reading, attending conferences, and participating in training. You need to seek opportunities whether you are a rookie or a veteran Sunday school leader. Are you where you need to be in your personal leadership at this point? If not, then you need to keep growing.

You have to keep going.

You may be tempted to apply a solution that absolutely guarantees failure. The only way you can fail is to give up, to quit, or to resign. Perhaps you want to move to another area of service because you are new and now realize that teaching a Sunday school class or small group is not what you are called to do. That would be appropriate if you sincerely believe that to be true. Some leaders, however, quit simply out of frustration. They do not transition to another area of service but stop leading altogether.

God has not called you to quit! God has called you to grow. You should seek to find the place of service that best fits your gifts and that is in keeping with what God has called you to do. Quitting is unacceptable. God gives every believer spiritual gifts for their employment in strengthening the body of Christ. Seek first to grow and improve in your leadership. You should transfer to the right place of service if you feel you have been misplaced. There will be times, however, when you will need to just step up and lead to meet a need in the body of Christ, even when it is not your preferred place of service. I believe small groups and Sunday school are critical strategies in leading the church in the fulfillment of the Great Commission. Step up or step over, but do not step down.

You have to keep sowing.

Are you leading your group to do outreach? An inwardly focused group will often stagnate. Go to the maternity ward at the local hospital and observe the families as they peek through the windows observing the joy of new life. The experience is anything but boring or uninspiring. When God blesses you or your group to play a role in bringing someone to new life that comes through trusting Christ as Savior your group will find great joy. It can be challenging and frustrating to lead a group to do outreach; however, the life of your group is affected by their focus. Keep the group focused outwardly and lead them to sow the seed continually. Who is the newest believer in your group? Pray that you can always point to someone new. New life in Christ will add life to your group!

CHAPTER 19

My Class Is Not Growing

✚ THE EMERGENCY

Does God want your group to grow? Do you understand that many Sunday school teachers and church members have no concern about the growth of your congregation or class? Leaders and members often say things that may sound reasonable to justify failure or lack of intentionality for the growth of the group or church. Here are some examples:

- I do not want our church or class to get too big.

- I do not think we should be out for numbers.

- I like our church or class the way it is.

- I like being part of a family church.

- I believe we should focus on going deeper.

- I am afraid those kids visiting our church are going to ruin our facilities.

- We pay the ministers to do the outreach.

- I believe we should focus on quality and not quantity.

- I won't be able to know everyone if our church gets too big.

Do you recall the imperative of the Great Commission? Jesus commanded that we "go and make disciples." Though the preceding list of statements may possess a sense of sentimental logic, they all stand in the way of the fulfillment of Christ's command. Does God want your group to grow? God wants people to have a personal relationship with Him by trusting Christ as Savior. The sacrifice of His Son Jesus on the cross bearing the sins of the world verified the depth of His love and the desire of His heart for people to come into a relationship with Him. The church and all believers have been given the mandate to share that news and to invite others to follow Christ, and as they do, both the church and your group grow. The question is not what do I think or what do I want, but what does God want? Go and make disciples.

✚ TRIAGE

1. Are you leading your class to engage in outreach?

2. Is your group seeking to bring people to Christ?

3. Are your leaders participating in training opportunities?

4. Are you expanding the enrollment of your group?

5. Are you providing an environment that challenges people to be obedient to Christ?

Diagnosis: Refer to page 17 to evaluate the severity of this emergency.

✛ PRESCRIPTION

Matthew 28:18–20	Ephesians 4:15–16
1 Corinthians 3:6	Acts 2:42–47

✛ FIRST AID

Do not apologize for wanting to grow.

You will find that not everyone wants the church or your group to grow. Many of them are well-meaning and do not understand that growth is not about larger numbers or about getting bigger. Growth is about people coming into a relationship with Christ and the church taking responsibility to assist them in their spiritual growth. Numbers increase as more people come into a relationship with Christ. Some members and maybe even some friends may try to make you feel some sense of guilt about wanting to grow. Always remember that Satan does not want the church or your group to grow either. Seek to obey God rather than to please men.

You have a responsibility for leading your class to be obedient to the Great Commission. Every group that does so will be blessed to see family, friends, and community members come into a relationship with Christ. Your group may not experience it every week or every month, but if you are obedient God will bless you to be a part of the process of people trusting Christ. Any guilt that a leader may feel for wanting the group or church to grow is not coming from God. He is daily bringing people into a relationship with Himself, and He allows people to be a part of His plan of reconciling sinners to Himself. Pray that the Lord will let you grow!

Apart from Christ, you can do nothing.

Moving forward, you will discover some of the practical strategies and principles for leading your class to grow. They are time tested and proven by churches and groups that experienced growth in their Sunday school ministries. However, application of the tools will not bear fruit without the work and the power of Christ in your life and the life of the group. The anointing of God on your ministry is not a principle but is essential and foundational. How are you doing in your personal relationship with Christ? Are you growing personally? Are you spending time daily with the Father? Are you filled with the Holy Spirit?

Volumes have been written and opinions are plentiful as to the reasons for the lack of growth and even the decline of churches and Sunday schools in recent years. However, you may have noticed that not every church or every group has stopped growing. Perhaps you are passionate and growing personally and yet not experiencing growth in your group. If that is the case then some of the more practical tools may help you in moving forward. Be absolutely sure that first and foremost you are seeking the power of God in your life and in your leadership. Empty yourself through repentance and then fill yourself with Christ by spending as much energy as possible in prayer, worship, and the study of God's Word.

It takes a team.

A team of leaders can obviously accomplish more than an individual, and a larger group will obviously require a larger number of leaders. Multiple leaders enable you to multiply the number of hours invested in ministry, the number of contacts with the unchurched, and the amount of ministry that can be done for the members. Having multiple leaders also maximizes the quality of ministry by utilizing the giftedness and passions of others. A team of six leaders can accomplish much more than an individual. You should give immediate attention to enlisting those who are attending to take on a specific role of leadership or ministry in partnership with you to strengthen and grow the group.

Do as Jesus exemplified in His enlistment of the apostles. Pray about who in your group is best equipped to help provide leadership and directly ask for their help. Remind those enlisted that you will work with them and that the ministry is a team effort. The time you invest is multiplied by many hours of service for each person brought on board. Consider who might help in the following areas:

- Organizational and administrative tasks

- Keeping the group focused on outreach and evangelism

- Planning fellowships that reach out to the unchurched and bring the group closer together

- Maintaining regular contact with all of the members

You will note that there are no titles and no flow chart. You choose titles for these roles based on your context and begin enlisting one by one in the recommended order as you see them presented. You can follow by having each of those leaders in turn enlist teams to assist them. The roles you see are not the only possibilities. Simply ask what it is that your class needs in order to be more effective, and then enlist members to focus on and lead in those areas.

There are some numbers that matter.

You may recall from the introduction that every paragraph could be a chapter and every chapter could be a book. The numbers that you are about to consider all affect the ability of your group to grow. You can find more details about implementing the following principles in *Sunday School That Really Works*.

1. You need to intentionally increase the enrollment. The average attendance will never exceed the enrollment and will ordinarily be between 40 to 60 percent. You will discover that the larger the enrollment pool the larger the attendance potential.

2. You need to intentionally increase the number of contacts made each week to members and prospects. The number of contacts affects the week-to-week attendance as much as anything else. Compare a group that extended twenty invitations and called every member absent last week with a group that invited one person and did not call those who missed. Which group is most likely to have strong attendance next week?

3. You need to increase the number of leaders serving in the class. More leaders enable you to accomplish more in your leadership.

4. You need to increase the number of prospects that your group has identified. Prospects are non-attending members, recent guests, and unchurched friends who are of the same life stage of your group and who are not enrolled or attending any other Bible study. The more people your group is praying for and inviting to fellowships and Bible study, the more the attendance can grow.

5. You need to be involved in increasing the number of classes or groups in your church. Twenty groups can reach and minister to more people than three groups. Sunday schools do not grow without increasing the number of classes. That means that you will have to cooperate and participate in helping your church create and launch new classes and groups in the future.

✚ REHAB

Become an expert.

What are the keys to growing a Sunday school class? If you have been reading this book all the way through, you should have a pretty good answer already. The challenge with growing a group is that there is not a single key but multiple keys. Leading a group to grow is more like opening a combination lock where several skills are needed.

Participating in training opportunities is critical at this point. You need to become the expert. Spend time in study, instruction, and application. Many Sunday school leaders feel as if they do not need training, but skill is simply a result of training and, sadly, many churches are filled with unskilled Sunday school leaders. How about you? Remember that as the expert in your class, the group will go where you lead them and they will not grow unless you lead the way.

If your church does not provide any formal training, you can increase your expertise in other ways. Seek out instruction. Reading a book like this is one way to accomplish the task. Do not stop here; also read *Sunday School That Really Works* as well as other books on Sunday school leadership. Check with your denomination or with other growing churches to discover what training opportunities they might have available. Call on someone who has proven effective and ask them to spend time coaching you personally. Expertise comes with time and investment. Recall that your growth must always be in the context of your spiritual development in order to make a difference for the kingdom. Becoming a good Sunday school leader will also help you to be a better leader at your place of employment and in your community. Commit to learn, develop, and apply the skills to take your group on a journey of growth.

Understand that increase will require decrease.

A growing group can develop momentum and will be very exciting. Very few things in life are as pleasing as seeing people come to know Christ and growing in their relationship with Him. What do you do if the group gets too large to manage or to maintain ministry to all of the members? Keep in mind that the church needs to create new groups in order for the congregation to grow. Your group is a prime candidate to assist in this cause if you are experiencing growth. Do not take offense when being challenged to create a new group. Taking members of your group to start a new group is quite a compliment. Taking members of a healthy group is a good strategy to ensure the health of the new group.

In addition, leaders will be needed in preschool, children's, and student ministries. One of the marks of a healthy and growing group is the spiritual health and growth of the members. You will need to release some of them for the benefit of the entire body or congregation. The growth of your group is not always reflected in total attendance. Your group may actually get smaller because of your intentionality in releasing members to assist and serve in other areas. The ultimate aim is the growth of the kingdom. Bring new people in as you bring them to Christ, lead them to grow and mature, and release them to serve. Kingdom growth will sometimes require that your increase result in a decrease.

CHAPTER 20

I Do Not Like the Curriculum

✛ THE EMERGENCY

Ten signs the curriculum will not work for you:

1. The curriculum is written in Hebrew or Greek.

2. The teaching plans call for the use of flannelgraph or filmstrips.

3. The teaching plans require the use of a live camel for an illustration.

4. The curriculum does not require the use of a Bible.

5. The curriculum has a 52-week series on fasting.

6. The curriculum requires a minimum PhD or equivalent to teach.

7. The curriculum requires preparation to begin at 5 a.m. Monday morning.

8. The teaching plans endorse polygamy.

9. The curriculum is written on stone tablets or in crayon.

10. The curriculum covers more than 66 books of the Bible.

✚ TRIAGE

1. Are you spending an appropriate amount of time in preparation each week?

2. Is the curriculum doctrinally sound?

3. Is the curriculum age-appropriate for the group you lead?

4. Does the curriculum cause the group to look into and study the Bible?

5. Is the curriculum designed so that new members and guests can get involved at any point along the way?

Diagnosis: Refer to page 17 to evaluate the severity of this emergency.

✚ PRESCRIPTION
2 Timothy 3:16; 2:15
Deuteronomy 6:1–9
1 Corinthians 9:19–23

✚ FIRST AID
Honor the convictions of your leaders.
You apparently did not choose the curriculum that you are currently using or this would not be an issue. The decision was made by your pastor, Sunday school director, or a leadership team from your church. Be cautious in the way that you approach your concerns. You want to be sure to do so in a way

that will not undermine key leaders in your church. You may have noticed that some people seem to think that they have the spiritual gift of criticism. While all believers should be free to express concerns and address issues, there are some members who have never heard of a decision that they liked.

Perhaps you do need to express concern, but you do not need to complain. The difference is in the attitude with which you express your feelings. In order to express a concern, you should identify the leaders responsible for the decision made about the particular issue. Seek to converse with those leaders about your concerns, questions, frustrations, or ideas. You seek some resolution and must rejoice if adjustments are made, accept if a reasonable explanation is provided, or proceed to do the best you can with what you have if circumstances remain as they are. Complaining, on the other hand, is expressed to anyone who will listen. They may not be able to do anything about it, but they empathize with you and make you feel more credible in your complaint. The problem is that those whom you serve as a leader will ultimately follow your example. Your attitude is critical to the effectiveness of your leadership, the health of your group, and the unity of your local church.

In addition, though your complaint is about the curriculum and not about a person, your complaining can have the unintended consequence of undermining the credibility of your leaders. Constant complaining suggests that your leaders do not know what they are doing. Be cautious. The point here is not to remain silent but to proceed with grace and wisdom.

Some leaders do not want to use any curriculum at all. They enjoy preparing and teaching their own material. That is generally not a problem so long as the studies are biblically sound and age-appropriate. However, they likewise can undermine the credibility of the church leaders if they plan their own lessons without the endorsement of church leaders. The curriculum is in place for a reason. It serves to keep everyone moving on the same track and can to some degree protect the congregation from the introduction of doctrine with which the church does not agree. Take the approach of preparing your own material only with the affirmation of church leaders and respectfully honor their wishes if they ask that a specific curriculum be utilized. You could likewise undermine your leaders by taking a rebellious approach. Do not take the admonition to utilize curriculum as an insult but as a decision made in the best interests of the congregation as a whole.

Examine the root of your concerns.

What is it that you do not like about the curriculum? Some Sunday school leaders do not like the curriculum because it is too hard to prepare. Keep in mind that the whole point of your teaching is to share insights as you lead the group to study God's Word and to apply it. The curriculum is intended to aid you in this important task. A prepared curriculum offers background research, summarizes historical and contextual information, and suggests activities and discussion starters to allow you to fast-forward your preparation of the Bible study for the week. Many hours have already been invested by the curriculum writers. Some do a more effective job than others, but they all save the Sunday school teacher time. Remember this key point: No lesson of significance will be preparation-free. Sunday school lessons will not prepare themselves, and though a curriculum will save you time, it will not eliminate the need for you to spend time in God's Word in personal preparation.

The curriculum should do the following:

1. Engage your group in the study of God's Word.

2. Support the inspiration and integrity of the Bible. (To do anything less is to make the Bible just another book

and will deter your group from commitment, study, or application.)

3. Be doctrinally sound.

4. Support the convictions and the missions strategies of your congregation.

5. Provide age-appropriate methods and ideas for your presentation.

6. Supplement your preparation and save you some time compared with preparing a Bible study or lesson totally on your own.

7. Allow for any guest or new member to begin participation at any point along the way.

8. Challenge participants to apply the message in their daily lives.

An absence of any of these characteristics is certainly a reason to express concern. Remember that good curriculum is not what makes the teaching good. It is a good teacher that makes the curriculum good. Be sure to examine the root of your concern before moving forward.

Converse with your leaders.

So, you have concluded that the issue is not that you are seeking preparation-free resources but that the curriculum is flawed because it is not age-appropriate, is not applicable, or does not meet one of the other needs previously suggested. The next step is perhaps obvious: set up a time to meet with your pastor, Sunday school director, or the appropriate staff member.

Take opportunity to listen to their reasons for selection of the current materials. You may find that there are alternatives, that there is openness to change, or that the current resources are being used with clear conviction and reason.

You should also be listening for what God may be saying to you through the process. You would do well to pray before you have the conversation, asking God to give you—as well as the leaders with whom you will be sharing—clarity, encouragement, and conviction. Are you willing to accept that God will intervene if needed or, if He does not intervene, that He may be teaching you a lesson? Commit to use whatever resources you have at hand to do the best that you can to teach God's Word each week and to make a difference in the life of your group.

✚ REHAB
Learn to use what you have.

The issue has been settled at this point. Perhaps there has been a change or maybe you know that the resources you currently have are the ones the church is committed to providing over the long term. Take some time to learn how to use the curriculum materials that you have. Your church leaders, denominational leaders, or the publishers of the curriculum likely have resources or training to help you to be more effective in the use of the materials. You may find that supplemental resources are available online from the publisher or from others who have encountered similar challenges and have taken time to develop and document solutions.

Identify other leaders from your church and from other healthy churches who use the same curriculum. Consider interviewing those leaders or perhaps ask for a season of mentoring as you seek to become better acquainted with the curriculum that you have. Participate in any and all training opportunities. The equipping provided by your leaders and the conferences provided by your denomination or other strong churches can enhance your ability to use any curriculum that you currently have access to. Read books or materials that directly focus on teaching as well as leadership. It is important to learn to use what you have because as important as the resources are, they are not the key. Teach from the overflow of your spiritual growth and develop skills to enhance your ability to present your message effectively.

Five keys to make it work.

1. Anointed Teaching: More than a better source of curriculum, you need the power of the Spirit of God to encompass your leadership and penetrate the lives of your group. Anointing is not reserved for pastors but is available to all who have access to the Holy Spirit. The anointing of God on your teaching enables you to present with passion and power in a way that affects your group beyond your abilities. Are you filled with the Holy Spirit? You must have an authentic and personal relationship with Christ that begins with a point in your life of repentance and faith. You then begin to walk with God and to grow in your relationship with Him through prayer, worship, the study of God's Word, and service with and through the body of Christ. Are you growing? Are you living a repentant life, keeping yourself pure before the Father? Are you spending time with God each day? What are you filling your life with? The most important thing you do for your group and the dynamic that will most affect your teaching is the level of intimacy that you have with Jesus Christ. That is the priority and is essential in order to experience God-anointed teaching.

2. Prepared Teaching: Busy? Yes, you are, but the task of leading a Sunday school class is not an "add-on" to your life.

It is a call to service for our Lord and King. It takes time and it takes sacrifice. I will not assign a specific amount of time that it requires, but I will say that the preparation cannot be done in a few minutes. I remember a teacher who once served in my ministry complaining that he did not have enough time to do the ministry to which he had committed and been called. This same teacher spent about two hours a day, five days a week, volunteering to coach youth sports. Now I have coached, and I appreciate that Christians need to be involved in these types of ministry and community opportunities. But I have to wonder what would have happened if this teacher invested ten hours a week in his Sunday school class. As much as I love sports, I must ask which of the two will have the most eternal significance. "I don't have the time" is not totally accurate. We all have the same amount of time. The issue centers on how we choose to expend it. You will not be effective unless you take time to prepare each week.

3. The Creative Advantage: It is not essential that you complete preparation early in the week, but it is important that you begin preparation several days ahead of time. I want to acknowledge again that you are a very busy person. You may find yourself completing preparation for Sunday's Bible study on Friday, Saturday, or even Sunday morning in some circumstances. That may not be ideal but it is a reality for a volunteer. You need to understand what I refer to as the "creative advantage." Creativity comes in proportion to the time that your brain has to process information. If you wait until Saturday to begin lesson preparation, you can get the job done but with minimum effectiveness. Preview your lesson as early in the week as possible. Take about fifteen minutes on Monday or Tuesday to preview next Sunday's plan, including the key passage, key application,

and suggested teaching activities. You will find that ideas will come to you as you go about your routine of life in the course of the week. You might hear a news story that will serve as a good illustration for your presentation. A discussion with another teacher during the week may prompt an idea for an age-appropriate activity for your class that reinforces the main point. You may recall an experience from your past that would serve as a good example of a point that you need to make. A Scripture that you read may apply to what you want to communicate. By the time you get to the actual preparation of the lesson later in the week, your brain has processed and developed several ideas that will enhance your presentation. The creativity that you will experience is a combination of spiritual insight and practical mental processes that will take your preparation and presentation to a new level of effectiveness.

4. Use Multiple Methods: You can see that Jesus used lecture as a method when you read Matthew 5–7. Is that the only method He used? Certainly not! He used parables, word pictures, debate, question and answer, illustrations, field trips, drama, object lessons, visual aids, projects, and stories. Why didn't Jesus, a master teacher, rely solely on lecture? As our Creator, Jesus understood that humans possess a variety of differing learning styles. The combination of methods enhances the ability of all members of the audience to learn and understand what is being taught. Application cannot occur if there is not understanding. The fact that Jesus used so many methods should influence our teaching approach. Any time that you teach, use three or four different methods. Do not fall into the trap of being a uni-method teacher.

5. Emphasize Application: Do not leave the Bible study without leading your class to discuss how the lesson of the

day should affect their lives. Bible study is not a philosophical or an academic exercise. It is an encounter with God the Creator, Christ the risen Lord, and the Holy Spirit. You cannot be neutral or passive about a word from God. Ask participants to share at the conclusion of the Bible study a testimony of what God has said to them and how they should respond. You could also conclude by asking everyone to get in groups of three or four and each take fifteen seconds to share what they need to do in light of what they have learned. You will be reinforcing the necessity of application when you prompt these testimonies and discussions as well as when you share your personal experiences.

CHAPTER 21

I Do Not Have Time to Lead My Class (to Do All That Is Needed)

✚ THE EMERGENCY

The only things that you need to do this week in order to be effective are:

1. Contact all members who were absent last Sunday.

2. Participate in the outreach ministry on Monday night.

3. Begin planning a fellowship for the group.

4. Visit a group member who is going through a crisis.

5. Attend the training session that's being held on Friday.

6. Enlist a replacement for a class group leader who recently moved.

7. Organize an upcoming mission activity for the group.

8. Read a book that your pastor recommended on leadership.

9. Enlist two group members to assist in preschool next week.

10. And [if I have time] prepare a dynamic lesson for the group on Sunday!

Note to self: I cannot do this by myself!

✚ TRIAGE

1. Have you been trained in your role as a Sunday school leader?

2. Have you ever received instruction in time management?

3. Are you purposefully organizing and enlisting others to help you?

4. Do you spend time leading your group to plan and organize when you meet each week?

5. Do you have a full sixty minutes or more with your group each week?

Diagnosis: Refer to page 17 to evaluate the severity of this emergency.

✚ PRESCRIPTION
Ephesians 5:15–17
Matthew 6:33
Exodus 18:13–26
Acts 6:1–7

✚ FIRST AID
Begin building a team.

An effective Sunday school class does more than conduct a Bible study each week. Ministry to all members, outreach to the unchurched, fellowship, engaging in missions, connecting new members, and working together to strengthen the church are the ways that the study of the Scripture is applied. You cannot possibly accomplish all of this by yourself. You need a team!

Where will you find the team that you need? They sit in the group with you each and every week. Your objective is to lead them to participate in accomplishing the aim of serving together in fulfillment of the Great Commission. All of the participants have talents and spiritual gifts that strengthen the body when exercised. They won't all have the same passions, interests, or gifts, but they do all have a variety of passions, interests, and gifts. They are available if you will begin to lead them in discovery and application of the gifts that God has given to each and every one. It will not be easy. The demands of the world and the negative influences of Satan and his demonic force will work against you to keep the members as complacent as possible.

The team needs to be organized. What do you need help with? What needs to be done? You have to prepare and present the Bible Study. What other things need to be happening each week? Make a list and prioritize according to importance. Start with one task and enlist one of the members to help you in that area. Don't stop until you have a team to help. It is an unending process and will not be done in a week, but you must get started because there is much to be accomplished by your group.

Begin leading instead of teaching.

It is possible to teach without leading. Leading means that you are influencing others. Your group members need for you to be a leader. They want someone who will motivate, challenge, and lead them in making a difference. Once you decide you will be a leader you will of necessity have to teach in order to accomplish your mission. Too many Sunday school classes have good teachers but are in need of good leaders.

You can prepare and present a lesson each week while only minimally interacting with those in your group throughout the weeks and months. A faithful core may attend and will likely live in complacency because of the lack of challenge experienced in your group. However, the group will not make a difference in your church and will not be blessed to see people come into a relationship with Christ. Jesus not only taught the disciples but also equipped them and led them to minister to those outside of the group. Leadership will require you to be attentive and intentional in organizing and leading your group to do ministry. Though it may appear as if this challenge will add extra time to your schedule, the opposite is true. Leadership that equips and brings others into the process will save you time over the long term because others will be sharing the load. The early investment of time made will multiply the amount of ministry done and minimize the burden on you to accomplish the many tasks of an effective Sunday school class.

Learn to enlist.

The next three paragraphs are repeated from a previous section of the book, but they apply here as well.

How was it that Jesus enlisted the apostles? Did He make a public announcement and ask people to sign up if interested? No. According to Luke 6:12, He prayed all night. As you study the New Testament account you will discover that He went and directly invited the apostles to follow Him.

Begin by praying about who should be the outreach leader for your class. Ask God to show you. Once He does you need to ask to meet with that person privately (not beside the welcome center in the hallway) or with you and your spouse or another group member if the person is of the opposite sex. Tell the individual that God has placed something on your heart that you want to share. When you meet, you should share what you have been praying about and what God has placed on your heart. Share two or three things that you need from an outreach leader (or whatever the role) and how long the commitment will be. You do not want an immediate answer; ask the individual to pray about helping in this area, and indicate that you will check back in a few days.

You will get one of three responses from the people you ask: (1) The individual will likely say yes, and you will have your leader. (2) The individual may say no, and you must trust that God either will deal with the disobedience or that He is leading in some other way. You have complimented the individual by asking, and God may be purposefully using your encouragement. (3) The individual may respond that he or she is not comfortable with outreach but wonder if there is some other way to help. That would be a blessing. The person might not have served at all had you not suggested the role of outreach leader. Enlisting directly in this manner is more time-consuming, but you will get better results because it is based in prayer and engages the Holy Spirit in the enlistment process.

Consider various options for enlisting help with children.

If you work with preschoolers, children, or youth, you may need to enlist one or more other adults to help you with your tasks. Don't discount the possibility of children and students accomplishing some of what is being suggested in response to helping you find more time. Some of the help you need may not require helpers to be in the group with you each week, although that would be ideal. You certainly need at least one adult assisting you with the class each Sunday, but do not pass up opportunities to enlist those who might help with a specific task or on an occasional basis. The key is to take responsibility for the enlistment. If you are waiting on others to enlist for you or for others to know what needs you have then you may be waiting a long time.

✚ REHAB
Develop and improve your time management skills.
Team enlistment is an important component of responding to this challenge, but you need to take time to evaluate and improve the management of your time. Sunday school teachers tend to be very busy individuals. They are called upon because they have proven themselves to be faithful and ordinarily have multiple leadership roles and responsibilities at church, at home, and in the community. Reading a book, attending a seminar, or visiting websites that provide time-saving tips is a worthy investment of your time. Several hours spent in this way may save you dozens of hours over the course of a year. In my previous book, *Sunday School That Really Works*, I shared some teacher time-management tips. Here is a summary of those ideas:

1. Utilize class time for organization. The best time to meet with your class and with leaders is when you have them all together. It is appropriate to spend about a quarter of your meeting time each week in fellowship, administration, and organizational functions. You will still have sufficient time for Bible study. You might also consider having "Leadership Day" once every four to six weeks. On those days, spend half your class time in planning and organization, leading the group to work together to apply what you have been teaching from God's Word. You will find more details on this idea as you continue to read.

2. Take advantage of Sunday lunch. I am in the habit of eating lunch each and every Sunday. How about you? Meet with

class leaders, teams, and/or potential leaders for lunch on Sunday. Taking one Sunday each month to meet with key members will add up to an investment of twelve to eighteen hours over the course of a year and will not infringe on any of your personal time.

3. Preview the next lesson by Monday night. Spend fifteen to thirty minutes looking over the Bible study for the following Sunday. What is the key passage? What is the lesson aim or objective of the study? What is the key application? Read the key passage alongside your devotions each day. Once you get into the actual preparation of the Bible study or lesson you may be surprised how much work your brain has done during the course of the week as you prayed, processed, and meditated on the upcoming presentation.

4. Utilize technology for meetings. Do you need to meet with a team or an individual to plan or organize some component of your ministry? Does it require face-to-face interaction, or could it be done some other way? Some tasks can be done by e-mail, by phone, or by some other means of electronic correspondence. These means allow participants to save the time of driving to the meeting and can eliminate some extraneous conversation. Wisely determine when personal gatherings are needed and when other means will suffice.

Place all members on a team.

A larger group can obviously have more teams and a smaller group will have fewer teams. Any group with an attendance of six or more could have three teams. For example, ask each group member if they would prefer to serve on the prayer team, share team, or care team. Please note that you do not ask if they want to serve but on which team they will serve. Some of your members may resist having all of the responsibility for a task or ministry but will willingly serve with a team. A team provides a safety net if an individual fears failure or feels un-equipped for the task.

You may appoint or ask each team to select a captain or coordinator. If you lead a larger group you may want to develop more teams. What should the teams do? The question is: what do you as the leader and the group you are leading need to get done? Developing teams is a wise way to engage your members even if you have enlisted leaders for the class. For example, if you have enlisted an outreach leader, a fellowship coordinator, a greeter leader, and a care group coordinator, you could ask each member to assist as team members with one of these leaders. Though the titles give a clue as to the focus of each team, you may need to communicate your expectations or allow the team to decide for themselves.

Conduct regular team meetings.

You may be wondering when in the world you would do this. The whole premise of this chapter is that you are already struggling with too much to do and not enough time to do it. I do have a solution for you. The best time for the teams to meet is when the group is already together. Your church would do well to provide at least seventy-five minutes from the time Sunday school begins until the worship service starts. A min-imum of sixty minutes allows the time to spend on Bible study and team coordination. However, no matter the schedule for your church you can take time during the actual Sunday school gathering to allow teams to meet.

Take a particular week of the month or, if you want the teams to meet less frequently, the fifth Sunday of the month each quarter. Scale back the amount of time spent on the Bible study for those particular weeks and give your teams ten to twenty minutes to meet, organize, plan, and strategize. Please understand that the Bible study is crucial and is not to be set aside or ignored. However, the Scripture does not commend a specific time frame for the study and a well-prepared, challenging study can be presented whether the teacher has fifteen minutes or forty-five minutes. Teams may certainly opt to meet at additional times and should be encouraged to do so. However, lead the teams to meet and plan, and ensure that it happens by taking advantage of the times when the group is already together.

CHAPTER 22

I Cannot Get Anyone to Help Me

✛ THE EMERGENCY

It is a great joy when you first hear your child declare, "I can do it by myself!" You invest your life and hundreds of hours to help them grow to some degree of independence. If all goes well they may be totally independent of you by the time they are about twenty . . . or twenty-four . . . or twenty-nine . . . or at least eventually. Likewise, you personally seek to live in such a way as to not be dependent on others. But it is an impossible task. God designed you to be interdependent in many ways. He wants you to depend on Him and He places you in situations throughout life where you have to depend on others.

Simple tasks and easy decisions can be handled on your own. The problem is that life is not always simple. You have been called and enlisted to be a Sunday school leader. Perhaps you were under the impression that it would not be very hard. Leading a group to grow spiritually and to reach out to those around them is a tremendous challenge. Participation is totally voluntary, and you do not have the leverage of a boss, a parent, a drill sergeant, or a police officer. You need help in order to accomplish all that is needed to lead the group to be healthy and growing.

You will not be able to lead the group effectively unless you get others to help. You will remember from chapter 16 the challenge that "no one wants to help with outreach." The challenge in this situation is more severe because no one wants to help do anything. Some of the solutions are found in chapter 16 and in the preceding chapter that addressed "I do not have time to lead my class." Therefore, this chapter will be brief, with a couple of additions to the former ideas.

✚ TRIAGE

1. Are you taking responsibility for enlisting others to help?

2. Are you praying for God to raise up leaders to help you?

3. Are you enlisting help directly (as opposed to general announcements)?

4. Does your group observe that you have a high level of commitment to the group?

5. Do you intentionally spend time on relationship building with the group?

Diagnosis: Refer to page 17 to evaluate the severity of this emergency.

✚ PRESCRIPTION
Luke 6:12–15
Matthew 9:9–10
1 Corinthians 12:1–31
Exodus 18:18–36
Matthew 9:37–38

✚ FIRST AID
Relationships are critical.

How long have you been leading your group? If you have just begun to lead a group, the fact that you are new may certainly be an issue. Imagine if a stranger walks up to you this afternoon and asks to borrow your car. Are you kidding me? There is no way you'd hand over the keys to your car. Suppose a close friend comes up and asks in desperation if he might borrow your car for a couple of hours. After some follow-up questions, you will likely grant his request. What is the difference between these two circumstances? It is the relationship that you have with each person.

How is your relationship with your group members? You do not even really have one if you are new. Begin investing time with the groups and individuals in the group. Be sure that you are spending time conversing when you are together on Sunday mornings. Plan for opportunities on some weekends when you can gather with group members informally to fellowship and recreate together. Make phone calls and schedule meals with individuals or couples in your group. Friends respond when their friends ask for help. Focus on building relationships.

Pray and pour.

"Then [Jesus] said to His disciples, 'The harvest truly is plentiful, but the laborers are few. Therefore pray the Lord of the harvest to send out laborers into His harvest'" (Matt. 9:37–38). Jesus acknowledged the challenge of getting people to help in kingdom service. He instructed the disciples to pray. Have you been praying for God to raise up leaders from among your group? Are you willing to release your members to do even greater things once they begin to assist you and to grow? Are you praying in faith and remaining committed to do whatever it takes to lead your group to be healthy and growing? Are you devoted to stay with the task and the fulfillment of your ministry until God gives you release?

Likewise you need to be pouring into your group as you are praying. Are you preparing Bible studies to feed the spiritual growth of your members and are you passionately delivering the content? You cannot bore people into commitment. Lead your members to grow in their relationship with Christ. They will not be able to sit on the spiritual sidelines if they are listening to the Holy Spirit, growing in their faith, and obeying the Scriptures. Jesus poured His life into the disciples, modeled compassion for the hurting, and led them to minister to believers and nonbelievers alike. Invest in the spiritual growth of your group while simultaneously building a stronger relationship with each member.

Be simple minded.

You may need to throw out the organizational chart for the time being. Organization and planning are of great value in leadership. However, the chart does no good if no one will help. As you are relationship building, praying, and pouring into the spiritual growth of the group, begin to ask for help. You may need to start with simple requests instead of asking for major commitments. Ask someone to attend outreach with you next week. Ask someone to make some phone calls for you next week. Ask someone to assist you with planning a fellowship for the group. Ask someone to bring some paper goods next Sunday. You will need to ask for someone to commit to serve as outreach leader, to serve as care group coordinator, to serve as the fellowship coordinator or perhaps the class hostess as you move forward. If you believe that you cannot get *anyone* to help, then you need to simplify and ask for smaller commitments. That will provide you with some of the help you need in the interim as you continue to develop relationships and build up the group through their spiritual development.

✚ REHAB
Invest in your leadership.

Have you had any leadership training? Leadership is nothing more than the task of influencing people. Your dilemma indicates either that you are new to the task or that you are struggling with your leadership. In either case you need to grow as a leader in order to maximize your influence. My favorite author on leadership is John Maxwell, and I recommend *Developing the Leader Within You*, a Leadership 101 book. You need to read something to sharpen your own leadership skills. Ask your pastor for suggestions. Perhaps he is aware of available training being offered through a seminar, conference, or some online source. Timothy had Paul to help him grow in his leadership. Do you have a "Paul" in your life whom you look to as a model and a guide to help you grow in your leadership? If not, find someone and seek his or her help. Finally, read this book cover to cover and read the preceding book, *Sunday School That Really Works*, and you will be a more effective leader when you are done. Invest in your leadership and you will maximize your influence, which in turn will result in the help you need.

Build a team.

The preceding chapter addresses this particular task, but I want to focus on one particular dynamic here. Be sure to read, or reread, chapters 16 and 21. Focus at this point on the word *build*. Have you ever built anything? Building is a process that requires incremental steps, persistence, and time. You do not begin building a house by nailing shingles to the roof but by establishing a firm foundation. The foundation of building a team is the spiritual growth, the prayer, and the relationships. The incremental steps involve first investing in those areas and then asking members to help with simple tasks. Persistence is required because you will experience setbacks and disappointments. You may want to give up at some point but you cannot. Why not? You cannot quit because God has called you to the task of growing and developing leaders through a Sunday school strategy. It will take time, and the task will not ever really be completed. If you could do this in a week or a month then volunteers would be standing in line. You may be thinking that it is hard to lead a Sunday school class or a small group. You are right, and if you are not frustrated you are not doing anything. Remember that it is worth all of the time and frustration because you are serving the King. Your leadership will make a difference in lives, not only for years to come but for eternity. Begin building a team.

CHAPTER 23

Our Leaders Expect Too Much of the Teachers

✚ THE EMERGENCY

I discovered many years ago the biggest lie of the Christmas season. Purchasing toys for your young children during the Christmas holiday season can be a joyous experience for a new parent. For the uninitiated you will discover that not all of the toys that your children desire arrive at your home fully assembled. Thus you will discover the biggest lie of Christmas. It is the disclaimer on the product that you purchase which states: "some assembly required." Somewhere around 2:00 a.m. after four to five hours of piecing together a dollhouse, bicycle, or some beloved toy, you begin to wonder why your child couldn't have made do with a Frisbee instead!

Somewhere between the one tool that you cannot find in your toolbox that is critical to the assembly, the instructions that require a degree in engineering to understand, the two parts that do not fit like the instructions suggest, and the four extra parts that are lying on the floor after you think you have fully completed the project, you swear to write your congressman requiring that such lies in advertising be outlawed. Nothing can describe the final insult and moment of panic as your child glides down the street riding what you have assembled when it hits you that those four leftover parts had something to do with the braking system.

Sunday school leadership sometimes comes with a lie of its own. Perhaps you were enlisted with the pitch that the role of Sunday school teacher would be easy. You were told of the rewards and the great resources that would be at your disposal. You had it covered because you had the latest curriculum, inherited an established group, and thought that a small amount of preparation and a half-decent Bible study delivery each week would barely take any of your time. You started with the illusion—whether directly communicated or from misguided perception—that "teaching Sunday school will be easy." What a lie! Now you have leaders who want you to attend training, to participate in outreach, to plan fellowships, to lead your class to start mission projects, and now to make matters worse, perhaps they want you to agree to standards and guidelines. How can leaders expect so much of volunteers? Our leaders expect too much of the Sunday school teachers. How should you respond?

✚ TRIAGE

1. Are your leaders trustworthy?

2. Do you have a good grasp of church health principles?

3. Do your leaders aspire to have a healthy Sunday school ministry?

4. Do you have a high level of personal commitment?

5. Are you committed to giving your best in fulfilling your leadership role?

Diagnosis: Refer to page 17 to evaluate the severity of this emergency.

✚ PRESCRIPTION
Romans 12:1–2
Titus 1:5–9
Ephesians 4:1–3

✚ FIRST AID
Do not fear or reject standards.

The expectations and the demands that you are experiencing may be implied, verbalized, or even written. You will best be served if they are written. Written guidelines and expectations strengthen the overall health of your Sunday school ministry in several ways.

First, the guidelines assist in getting all leaders on the same page. The expectations are equitably applied because all leaders are serving under the same level of expectations.

Second, the guidelines give you recourse if or when your leaders ask too much. You can go back to what was agreed upon based on what is written in black and white and are less likely to be blindsided by some additional requirement that you never knew about.

Third, the leaders can more effectively address weaknesses and deal with ineffective leaders. You are assisting your leaders by cooperating with the guidelines. They provide an objective way for church leaders to deal with the difficulties they occasionally encounter.

Fourth, the guidelines improve the quality of the Sunday school ministry. It is simply a fact that Sunday school ministries that have agreed-upon standards of leadership are stronger and healthier than those that leave expectations to everyone's own imagination. Rather than fearing written guidelines, you would do well to insist on them in order to ensure that everyone has a clear grasp of what is expected.

Do not be afraid to seek help.

Are there no clear written guidelines and expectations? Go to your leaders and work together to develop four to six points of agreement to be used in clarifying what is expected of leaders. Do you have guidelines that ask too much of Sunday school leaders? Go to your leaders and discuss reasonable expectations that will not compromise the health of the ministry or the ability to be obedient in fulfilling the Great Commission. Are your leaders asking you to do things that were not communicated when you were enlisted? Go to your leaders and discuss your initial commitment and the guidelines that you received at the outset. Are you struggling because you do not know how to do what is being asked of you? Go to your leaders and discuss an equipping plan to provide you with the needed skills.

Perhaps the expectations and guidelines are reasonable but you are struggling with application because of conflicts with time and other responsibilities. Go to your group members and other adult leaders to seek their wisdom and personal assistance in fulfilling the obligations that you have. You belong to the body of Christ. The Sunday school will not be effective if the leaders have low levels of commitment or if they do the minimum in order to just get by. A balance exists when you commit to do what is needed and you understand that it is never intended that you do it alone. Do not be afraid to seek help.

Do not overextend yourself.

How many ministries are you involved in? Sunday school leaders ordinarily represent some of the most committed leaders in the congregation. Therefore, they are often called upon to participate and lead in many ministries. Be on guard at this point. You can participate in more than one ministry and be effective, but you cannot participate in several. The difficulty is that you will give some effort to all of them but fail to give your best to any of them. I am going to suggest to any who read this book that you release something other than your Sunday school leadership. In the context of the work of the Holy Spirit I must tell you that the health of the church is largely built on the Sunday morning ministry, and Sunday school is a critical component of Sunday mornings. Sunday school grows disciples, ministers to members, connects new believers, reaches out to the unchurched, and develops leaders. No other ministry accomplishes so much in the context of a single strategy.

The challenge may not be that your leaders expect too much but that you have overextended yourself. Coaching little league, serving on the kitchen committee, playing golf twice a week, or watching twenty hours of television weekly can all be enjoyable and in some cases can have a positive influence. These four examples are merely representative of the hundreds of activities that vie for your attention. But please remember this: leading the Sunday school ministry is an investment in lives. The investment has an eternal consequence, and the one person you touch has the potential to ripple outward touching dozens and even hundreds of lives for many years to come. Few activities exist that will afford you the opportunity to affect lives while serving Christ as will leading a Sunday school class or small group.

✦ REHAB
Do not be afraid to wrestle.

Ministry is rarely an easy endeavor. Serving Christ and getting involved in the lives of growing believers, volunteers, people in crisis, complainers, and the unchurched is often frustrating, time consuming, and distracting from the much easier alternative of minding your own business. God did not call you to be a hermit but to be salt and light to a world in desperate need of God's love and grace.

You will find yourself wrestling to get people involved, to get the help you need, and to participate in the fellowships you plan. You will also struggle to meet the expectations of your leaders, to get people engaged in outreach, to get people to make and to follow up on commitments. You are not alone. Every leader wrestles with these challenges and often lives in a perpetual state of frustration. Then someone trusts Christ as Savior. Then someone says thank you for investing in his or her life. Then someone makes a wise decision that improves his or her life because of the wisdom that you shared. All of the sudden you realize that it was worth wrestling for weeks, months, or even years to be used by God to touch someone's life. The problem is not that you are wresting with these things. The problem would be if you failed to wrestle with them. Life sure would be easier for you if you simply let everything go. But, someone is waiting on you to touch his or her life through your leadership. Do not stop wrestling. You have divine appointments awaiting you.

Do not neglect to build a team.

Now that the book is nearing conclusion, you can see that some items come up repeatedly. You should give added attention whenever that happens and prioritize those elements of your leadership. Turn back and read or reread the concluding section from the preceding chapter about team building. That section will in turn refer you to other chapters where this issue has been addressed. That is the nature of emergencies in life as well as in Sunday school leadership. People have to work together to respond to and resolve difficulties and crises. It may be that what you see as an emergency, God sees as an opportunity.

CHAPTER 24

I
Want
to Quit

✚ THE EMERGENCY

Resignation Mad Lib: Ask a friend to give you a random word or phrase as prescribed for each bracket. Type it up and give it to your pastor or Sunday school director. Once he has read your resignation and you are both done laughing, tear up the resignation letter and get back in there!

Dear [**Pastor's Name**]:

I hereby tender my resignation as Sunday school teacher at [**name of church**] as of [**today's date**]. It has been my pleasure to teach Sunday school for the past [**number from 1 to 50**] years. I had [**hair color**] hair when I started and now it's [**choose: bald, gray, a mullet, shaved, or unmanageable**].

I decided last [**a holiday**], after one of my members brought [**a food item**] for our class breakfast wrapped in [**an animal**] skin, that I would soon resign. The odor was like [**something that smells strong**] and I could hardly teach my lesson. The text for the day was [**favorite Bible** text] but the discussion centered totally around [**repeat food item above**] and [**favorite TV show, sport, or historical figure**]. You know that I am more serious-minded than the group that I have, and I cannot tolerate this situation any longer. When you add this event to [**craziest thing you've ever heard of happening in a Sunday school class**], and the fact that the director is trying to [**something Sunday school teachers/classes typically resist**], I have had it up to my [**a body part**] and cannot take it any longer. I am turning in my curriculum, my roll book, and my [**item found in an attic**].

Good luck finding my replacement. You often have referred to me as the [**a superhero**] of our Sunday school, but I must take leave or I will [**something that happens when someone gets sick**].

Sincerely,
[**your name**]

✚ TRIAGE

1. Are you growing in your faith?

2. Do you have a desire for your church to be healthy and vibrant?

3. Have you been purposefull in developing your leadership skills?

4. Do you have a high level of commitment?

5. Are you committed to giving your best in fulfilling your leadership role?

Diagnosis: Refer to page 17 to evaluate the severity of this emergency.

✚ PRESCRIPTION
2 Timothy 4:1–8
Matthew 28:18–20
Hebrews 12:1–2

✚ FIRST AID
Clarify what you mean by "quit."

I was once speaking to a teen whose dad was upset because she was "quitting" softball. Her statement took me by surprise, not because she was quitting, but because she was sharing this with me in the winter when no softball leagues were playing. She had played many seasons and was tired of the sport and wanted to spend more time with her passion for music. The reality was that she was not quitting softball but that she would not be playing in the upcoming season. There is a difference between quitting and not recommitting. One of my daughters wanted to quit a sport in mid-season one time. I did not allow it because she had made a commitment and I did not want her to think it is ever acceptable to quit. However, I left it to her discretion once the season was complete if she wanted to re-commit for another season.

Here is my point: You must complete your obligation. Do you mean that you intend to quit, which is something that is more abrupt and more difficult on your church and leaders, or that you do not plan to recommit once the cycle is complete? I am not suggesting that you do not need to recommit but that it would not be the equivalent of "quitting." Read on, however, before making a final decision.

Clarify your reason.

Why is it that you do not want to continue to teach Sunday school? Tell your reason to God and sincerely seek to determine if your reasoning is acceptable to Him. Do not make excuses or try to justify your reasons in your own mind. Above all else you need release from God because He is ultimately the one who called you. There are right reasons and wrong reasons to discontinue your role as a Sunday school teacher. Right reasons include:

- Illness (yours or a family member's) that prevents you from fulfilling obligations

- Moving to another community

- After your first year of teaching you sincerely understand that you are in the wrong area of service for your giftedness

- You have been conducting yourself in such a way that the reputation of Christ or your local church could be harmed

- God has called you to another ministry that conflicts with your Sunday school leadership responsibilities

What are some wrong reasons to discontinue? Here are some examples:

- You are upset with someone in the church or got your feelings hurt

- The leaders want to change your class by asking you to change locations, release members to serve, or to start a new class

- The leaders have high standards for Sunday school leaders

- The class/group is not going well right now

- You just do not feel like doing it anymore

Be sure that your reasons are spiritual and not selfish. It is not supposed to be easy, and few ministries that make a significant difference are easy. You cannot expect to be in a leadership role that is totally free of frustration, challenge, difficulty, or sacrifice. That is why many are not willing to step up to a leadership role. Do you have a real conflict that prevents you from serving in the role, or are you looking for an easier path? Teaching Sunday school is a challenging task. Plenty of people are available for the easier assignments in your church. Do not quit unless you really have to.

If you must, then quit the right way.
Take note of a few quick dos and don'ts:

- Do not quit without notice, except in a severe emergency situation. That is unethical and leaves your church and leaders in a terrible position. Should you not be able to complete your commitment give a minimum of four weeks' notice.

- Do not quit without resolving personal disputes. No matter whether you continue or stay, it is critical that you repair any divisions, offer and seek forgiveness, and take the high road in the most spiritual sense.

- Do not cause division in the body. If you are upset with someone or some circumstance, be careful not to create division by overreacting or addressing the situation inappropriately.

- Do not quit without a plan to serve elsewhere. Not serving is not an option for a follower of Christ. The question for the believer is not whether to serve but where to serve.

- Work with your leaders on procedures. If you must discontinue serving, ask and follow church expectations as closely as possible.

- Debrief with your leaders to enable them to help future Sunday school teachers.

✛ REHAB
There are things you cannot do.

First, you cannot drop out of church once your commitment is complete. Imagine the message that is sent to those you have been leading to grow spiritually and to follow Christ if you not only quit serving but totally stop attending. I have seen this happen, and it is tragic. You may be disappointed, upset, or simply tired. However, you do not need to allow your faith to go in reverse and potentially devalue all that you have been teaching your group about their faith and spiritual growth.

Second, you cannot stop serving. Every believer possesses one or more spiritual gifts that come from Christ and are given for your employment in serving God. The application of your gifts serves to strengthen the body of Christ and make your congregation healthier and more effective in reaching the unchurched. The message to those who followed you will be discredited if you do not continue to apply what you were teaching whether as a Sunday school leader or in some other leadership role unless you are literally physically hindered.

Third, you cannot leave without resolution. If your departure from leadership or from your local church is because of disagreement or conflict, you have a biblical and spiritual obligation to seek reconciliation. Offer and seek forgiveness whether it is quick and easy or requires counsel and deliberation. Remember that your former group members are still learning about faith as they observe how you handle difficult issues.

Get to your post.

So, you are no longer going to teach Sunday school? Your reasons may be legitimate, and I trust that you are following God's leading. As you follow His leading, follow Him to your next place of service. Every believer has a role in the body of Christ. Read Ephesians 4:11–16. Every believer according to the Scripture should be connected to a local body of believers and should be exercising gifts in service to Christ along with the family of faith. It may be appropriate to shift or to move to another ministry, but the Holy Spirit will not let you quit serving the Christ who saved you and called you into His service. Get to your post.

SOME CLOSING THOUGHTS

ONE OF THE CHALLENGES OF leading a congregation is that you face some challenges that you honestly can never conquer. Though the list is not exhaustive, I want to give you five examples. Each of these applies to pastors, staff, and all Sunday school leaders. The first is the area of evangelism. You cannot make an announcement, provide a seminar, preach a sermon, or do anything that will bring the challenges of evangelism to a conclusion. You must give continual attention to evangelism year in and year out in order to bear fruit. You will notice that when it is neglected, individuals coming into a relationship with Christ through the ministry of your congregation amount to few or none. I personally like to have a task, go after it, and get the job done. The task of evangelism is never finished, and it is essentially unconquerable. Do not grow weary or else you may miss a season of great harvesting.

Likewise, spiritual development, small group ministry (Sunday school), guest friendliness, and enlistment of leaders can never be conquered. The body of Christ will suffer if you neglect any of these, and even if you assertively engage them you will never come to an end of the task. Yet, the Scripture exhorts us not to grow weary. You must find a way to attend to each of these areas of ministry while understanding that you do have options:

1. "Do it" yourself. Sometimes that is necessary when you are beginning a ministry or in a very small setting.

2. "Delegate the task" to someone else. That is a viable option and is logical if you are blessed to have staff or several leaders already in place.

126665

3. "Initiate it." You provide the direct hands-on leadership to get the ministry moving with the intent of handing it off within a matter of weeks or a few short months. Jesus modeled this approach in His leadership of the apostles.

4. "Develop a team" to address the task at hand. In this circumstance you enlist others to work alongside. You are directly involved but share the load with others whom you enlist, train, and meet with regularly. Sunday school ministry and Sunday school groups work best with this model.

Remember, that the task will never be complete. Don't grow weary, and continually seek God's wisdom for confronting the challenges that arise. May God richly bless you in leading a Sunday school that really responds.